From Critical Theology to a Critical Theory of Religious Insight

american
university
studies

Series VII
Theology and Religion

Vol. 250

PETER LANG
New York • Washington, D.C./Baltimore • Bern
Frankfurt am Main • Berlin • Brussels • Vienna • Oxford

Marc P. Lalonde

From Critical Theology to a Critical Theory of Religious Insight

Essays in Contemporary Religious Thought

PETER LANG
New York • Washington, D.C./Baltimore • Bern
Frankfurt am Main • Berlin • Brussels • Vienna • Oxford

Library of Congress Cataloging-in-Publication Data

Lalonde, Marc P.
From critical theology to a critical theory of religious insight:
essays in contemporary religious thought / Marc P. Lalonde.
p. cm. — (American university studies VII:
Theology and religion; vol. 250)
Includes bibliographical references and index.
ISBN 978-0-8204-8609-3
ISSN 0740-0446

Bibliographic information published by **Die Deutsche Bibliothek**.
Die Deutsche Bibliothek lists this publication in the "Deutsche
Nationalbibliografie"; detailed bibliographic data is available
on the Internet at http://dnb.ddb.de/.

The paper in this book meets the guidelines for permanence and durability
of the Committee on Production Guidelines for Book Longevity
of the Council of Library Resources.

© 2007 Peter Lang Publishing, Inc., New York
29 Broadway, 18th floor, New York, NY 10006
www.peterlang.com

All rights reserved.
Reprint or reproduction, even partially, in all forms such as microfilm,
xerography, microfiche, microcard, and offset strictly prohibited.

Printed in Germany

For Michael and Benjamin

Contents

Acknowledgments ix

Introduction
From Critical Theology
To A Critical Theory of Religious Insight:
Essays in Contemporary Religious Thought 1

Essay One
From Postmodernity to Postorthodoxy,
Or Charles Davis and the Contemporary
Context of Christian Thought 15

Essay Two
Power/Knowledge and Liberation:
Foucault as a Parabolic Thinker 29

Essay Three
On the Moral-Existential Facet
Of Religious Studies Today 45

Essay Four
Fragments of Religion:
An Exercise in Critical
Post-Religious Thought 65

Essay Five
A Critical Theory of Religious Insight 81

Conclusion 101

Bibliography 105

Index 117

Acknowledgments

I WOULD like to thank the editors of the various journals who gave special permission to reprint the following essays in this volume: "From Postmodernity to Postorthodoxy, Or Charles Davis and the Contemporary Context of Christian Theology," *Studies in Religion/Sciences Religieuses* 22/4 (1994): 43-7–449; "Power/Knowledge and Liberation: Foucault as a Parabolic Thinker," *Journal of the American Academy of Religion* 61/1 (1993): 81–100, by permission of Oxford University Press; "On the Moral-Existential Facet of Religious Studies Today," *Studies in Religion/Sciences Religieuses* 26/1 (1997): 25–43; "Fragments of Religion: An Exercise in Critical Post-Religious Thought," *Philosophy, Culture, and Traditions* 3 (2005): 134–153; "A Critical Theory of Religious Insight," *Studies in Religion/Sciences Religieuses* 34/3–4 (2005): 357–374. With some slight alterations, most of the essays appear here in their published form. The "Introduction" and the "Conclusion," however, are original to this work.

Many of the essays in this volume were originally presented in the Department of Religion Colloquium Series, Concordia University. I would like to take this opportunity to thank my colleagues for their helpful comments regarding these papers. Along these lines, I would like to express a special note of thanks to Michel Despland for his very perspicacious suggestions for "A Critical Theory of Religious Insight," and to Michael Oppenheim—teacher, friend, and colleague—for his ongoing contribution to the development of my ideas.

A very special thanks is also owed to the Concordia Institute for Canadian Jewish Studies (Dr. Norman Ravvin, Chair) and to the Office of the Vice-Provost, Research (Dr. Vo-van, Vice-Provost), Concordia University, whose generous support helped to make the publication of this volume possible.

Finally, I would like to thank my wife, Beverly, who took time from her much deserved summer vacation to help me prepare this manuscript for publication.

Marc P. Lalonde
November 1, 2006
Montréal

Introduction

From Critical Theology to a Critical Theory of Religious Insight:
Essays in Contemporary Religious Thought

WHAT, PRECISELY, is critical religious thought? Why is it important? Why bother cultivating such a form of religious thinking? Does it contribute anything worthwhile to the development of contemporary thought? Does it deepen our comprehension of the present? Does it allow for a specific relation to a particular religious tradition? Or might it demand the adoption of a more general approach to religion *as such*? If so, is the thought at stake sufficiently historical and concrete? If not, is it sufficiently critical? In brief, why should the religious thinker be at all moved by its analyses? And why should the non-religious thinker pay it any mind?

These are just some of the questions and concerns that are addressed in this small but, I hope, engaging book of programmatic essays on the movement from "critical theology" to, what I am calling, "a critical theory of religious insight." To be sure, the ensuing investigations hardly exhaust the topic and represent but one way to cultivate this field of study. Yet as trial explorations they are demanding of thought. There is a bringing together of disparate sources and disciplines; an odd mixture of opposed languages and terms; and a concentrated labour to expand upon curious associations. What emerges is a tentative proposal about what religious thought *could be*. This is not to hint at the prospect of a radical *novum*. Nothing absolute begins nor ends with this project. Still, its inspiration is speculative and its goal experimental as it *pursues the religious as conceptual resource for theoretical innovation*—"to think otherwise"[1] requires at least a modicum of risk.

Critical religious thought comes to the fore after a relatively prolonged—if not entirely effective—encounter with critical theory. By "critical theory" I not only intend the contribution of western Marxism, the Frankfurt School or Jürgen Habermas, central as they are. Along side these sources we now must add post-structuralism and postmodernism, feminist critique and literary theory, to name but a few key forms of theoretical advance. This recent explosion of theory within western culture has undoubtedly meant an enrichment of critical-theoretic possibilities.[2] Its polyphonic character has encouraged a stimulating juxtaposition of different voices and rhetorics, helping to sound strange new themes that might otherwise remain mute.[3] While religious thought has been too quiet for too long, the clash and contrast of multiple theoretical approaches modify that unhappy predicament by presenting variable tasks to perform.

What, then, are the tasks that issue from this highly diverse, more open theoretical situation for religious thought today? How does this shift square with critical theory? How will it justify the standing of critical religious thought? And, most importantly, will such a form of thought be truly critical while bringing to bear a duly complex religious inspection that promises fresh insight?

From Critical Theology…

As a first step toward answering these questions, it might be helpful to compare and contrast "critical theology" on the one hand, with the understanding of critical religious thought and theory unfolding in this volume, on the other. These two approaches or interpretative strategies, as it were, are not quite the same, even if there exists a notable degree of historical and thematic overlap. Still, clarifying their difference will help to flesh-out the unique potential of critical religious thought today.

As I have analyzed it in more detail elsewhere,[4] critical theology represents an effort to "modernize" theological thought by appropriating the work of Karl Marx, the Frankfurt School, or Jürgen Habermas, to cite only the most prominent cases. One of the broad aims of this appropriation is to furnish Christian thought with a critically effective relationship to contemporaneity. Indeed, to be "critically effective" and "contemporary" is absolutely central to this theology. For Christianity *must*, it seems, be critically effective—socially, culturally, politically, intellectually—if its saving message is to be at all valid for the present time, that is, if it is to be truly "saving" at all. This weighty theological concern is played out in relation to critical theory in at least two ways—

First, there is a *conservative* endeavour by some to secure the critical effectiveness of Christian theology by asserting its absolute necessity for critical theory.[5] Theology is here advanced as fundamental to the meaning and development of critical theory. Failing a substantive injection of theological content, critical theory would somehow cease to be critical. Via this circuitous route, theology appears as always already critical and, therefore, as always already effective and contemporary. The saving message was never in serious peril after all.

Second, a much more *radical* theological approach to critical theory concludes with some far-reaching changes for theological thought and method.[6] Indeed, it is this particular line of attack that characterizes my initial foray into critical religious thought through the work of Charles Davis, Michel Foucault, and Liberation Theology (essays one and two in this volume). While these examinations represent important stages in the construction of a critical religious thinking and theory, the depth and range of their particular self-critique is so trenchant that it presages the demise of theology altogether. An elemental question arises here: why then bother with critical theology at all? Why not simply embrace critical theory and be done with it? Alas, this deduction exacts too much. Theology tends to return through the back door by a highly fluid, undogmatic faith that posits its identification with the critical operations of thought. This theological appropriation of critical theory can then be understood as an expression of a critical faith working on itself as faith. As a result, its radical revisions alter nothing essential as the *kerygma* effectively reaches us in the form of sophisticated theory. Once again, the Christian saving message lives to see another day.

Obviously the above synopsis intends to single out a specific difficulty: the apologetic purpose of what passes as "critical" theology.[7] Here a theological agenda is foisted upon a critical theory that simply does not share, embody, nor articulate the Christian faith in any substantial way.[8] Similarly, the priorities of critical theory seem equally forced upon a theology that does not—perhaps cannot—shoulder the exigencies of critical theory. The radical theological appropriation of critical theory proves the point as the very discipline of theology is put on the chopping block in the process. The fact that it is saved by a critical form of faith is but a short-term solution that foreshadows its long-term dissolution. In effect, both critical theological strategies represent a rather plain exercise in identity thinking that requires an ontological sameness to hold between the terms of relation lest the correlation be deemed invalid. Either critical theory must already *be* theological, or theology must somehow already *be* critical. Short of this identification, the fusion of their respective horizons cannot be fully executed.

Now, one cannot help but sense a real degree of anxiety at work within the modern Christian struggle to secure its validity as critically effective and its status as contemporary. In terms of the historical context and trajectory of contemporary religious thought, this struggle is not without significance. The distress at work here partially stems from the confrontation between the traditional historicization of the eschatological as universal mission, on the one hand, and the dawning of the post-Christian situation which radically limits or negates this mission, on the other. The post-Christian predicament, says Doug Hall, refers to the fact that "Christianity has arrived at the end of its sojourn as the official, or established religion of the Western world. The churches resist coming to terms with this ending, because it seems a dismal thing."[9] Many Christians view this situation as an instance of debilitating marginalization with certain disempowerment. This perception has elicited various reactions: conservative fundamentalism, liberal compromises that result in the privatization of faith,[10] the short-lived (but still germane) "death-of-God" theology,[11] or the postmodern celebration of religious collapse and the prospect of wholesale renewal.[12] In each case—including the most iconoclastic examples of Christian thought—there abides that effort to place Christianity at the centre of things cultural, societal, or political. At the same time, though, the very scope and character of these multiple responses betray the post-Christian fact that the Christian tradition is but one species of religious life within a more general religious sub-culture positioned, in its turn, by a many-sided secular environment. In effect, Christianity—or better, "christianities"—are but one form of religious tradition among many, engulfed by a sea of non-religious forms of thought and life. The socio-cultural or political context does not exist to support any exclusive claim to "Revelatory Truth" or religious supremacy. As a result, Christian thought—like religious thought as a whole—is strained to become more modest.

Toward that end, it is necessary to abandon that struggle to force the amalgamation of religion and critical theory and, instead, to articulate another model of affiliation altogether. This model will have to reconsider the current socio-cultural and religious milieu in which the affiliation comes to be; to undercut the religio-idealist urge to impose identity or fusion as the fundamental theoretical goal; and to eagerly explore how this new religious and theoretical *fragility* may yet conclude with a vigilant form of critical theory with notable religious weight.

Yet don't even these suggestions echo the Christian uneasiness over its socio-cultural marginalization? The entire notion and development of a critical religious thinking hints at this troubled heritage. I will not deny this pressure: critical religious thought, as I am trying to sketch it out here, has been partially shaped by modern Christian thought in general, and by critical theology in particular.[13] One might therefore pose the following question: can the distress over the development of a critical religious thinking today be immanently shared by another tradition, in another historical, socio-cultural context, in exactly the same way? Perhaps not. This is not to deny the existence of other forms of critical religious thinking. As my critique of critical theology suggests, I do not intend to hold fast to the Christian contribution to critical religious thought (even as certain Christian themes and concerns come to the fore during analysis). There are numerous other traditions that impel the unfolding of a critical religious thinking: the full gamut of disciplines that make up religious studies; the assortment of modern and postmodern secular philosophies; and, more specifically, the diverse expressions of modern Jewish thought. Still, it seems equally true that the Christian tradition intervenes in a special way and constitutes the "spiritual backdrop"[14] that helps to shape this project—the "view from nowhere"[15] is not on. The fundamental sight-lines that steer the course for a contemporary critical religious thinking, however, do not aim to make thought and theory more Christian. The end-goal is to bring religious thought to bear *as religious* in order to extricate contemporary thought from itself; to open up new horizons of interpretation; to generate innovative ideas; and to establish the basis for "A Critical Theory of Religious Insight."

What, more specifically, does this theory involve?

To A Critical Theory of Religious Insight…

To begin on a negative note—a critical theory of religious insight is not to be achieved by imposing religious themes or concepts on to existing forms of critical theory. To do so might supply a religious flavour to Habermas' "theory of communicative action" or to Adorno's "negative dialectics," for example, but there can be no integral synthesis. There cannot because the religious concern as religious seldom survives the intense, comprehensive character of critical theory as it absorbs the religious point into itself. True enough, this point is sometimes recognized as an interesting datum for critical theory insofar that the religious attaches itself to other phenomena in need of critical redress.[16] The derivative character of this association, moreover, is not without creative impetus. A religious moment may periodically surface and linger in such a way that its strangeness intimates a discarded element of social life with critical potential. Without denying the significance of this peculiar connection, one still cannot conclude an intrinsic religious interest. To do so would either do violence to the religious content at stake or to the content of critical theory. While we are not dealing here with incommensurable theories, it remains highly doubtful that there can be any justifiable "theory of *religious* communicative action" or "*religious*-negative dialectics," or what have you. At most there could be a theory of communicative action or negative dialectics with a very weak religious impulse. However, that impulse will always remain bound to a critical theory that, in the final analysis, does not need the religious moment to be critical.

Having said that, it does not follow that this problematization authorizes a highly aggressive form of critical religious thinking either. There can be no suggestion of a critical religious thought that inevitably overcomes all secular forms of critical theory. Oddly enough, the prevalence of a cultural and philosophical nihilism has encouraged just that. In this case, the postmodern struggle among competing, free floating narratives endorses the advance of religious narrative over against its secular competitors as but another move in a language game devoid of independent evaluation. After all, if reality is shaped by the kinds of stories we tell, then why not displace the secular story with the more solicitous Christian or Islamic or Jewish story etc., as the baseline for what counts as real or true? Regardless of what some of these "post-nihilistic" religious thinkers contend, the sub-text of this discourse is power and domination.[17] This by itself suggests its secular parallel and rank rather than any genuine religious surpassing.

How, then, a critical theory of religious insight?

Put positively, critical religious thought, as critical, looks to constructively expand upon extant forms of critical theory (via the creative mediation of religious *and* non-religious sources of knowledge) so as to produce a distinct—though never completely independent—form of critical theory. The point of entry—and only the point of entry—for this extension entails the examination of carefully selected ideas, themes, or values in critical theory that appear to call for a religious intercession or cultivation. Such a selection, of course, is hardly self-evident nor final. Complex argument and interpretation are required. However, to anticipate some possible candidates for critical-religious work we can mention: the prohibition against representing the Absolute; the critical-theoretic regard for love and compassion; and the interest in the elimination of social injustice, etc.[18] Such *conjunctures*, it should be stressed, must not be confused with a shared foundation nor matching telos. Any hint of essentialism is eschewed in favour of a more conditional, but no less comparable, connection: namely, the unforced crossing of religious fragments with key critical concerns that aptly lend themselves to critical-religious development.

Such conditionality does not connote sheer arbitrariness. The delicate overlap of critical-theoretic and religious concerns can be explained, though such deliberation will always be limited and incomplete. Yet such indefiniteness is not necessarily an impediment to further thought but rather an opening for a more extended reflection.

To unpack the details of this claim a bit further—

The emission or issue of averted religious contents to secular forms of thought—like critical theory—need to be mapped out in relation to our post-religious situation. By "post-religious" I do not mean the total obfuscation of religious language, thought, experience, etc., from the reservoir or reach of human meaning. This is neither possible nor desirable. The term "post-religious" rather denotes the secular deflation and separation of religious worldviews that entail the acknowledgement of multiple religious traditions and streams within each tradition. In such a fractured context, religious culture is always a sub-culture. Yet as a sub-culture, religion is simultaneously an exposed sub-culture—that is, necessarily interacting with and engaging the complexity of the world at large. There thus transpires an unpredictable, intractable overflow of religious contents to explicitly "other" cultural frameworks. The result? Religious traditions splitting away from themselves, becoming otherwise than revered, sacred or holy, and indiscriminately releasing a destabilized religious substance into ever wider circles of non-religious life and thought.[19]

Might this outcome be explained as the infamous "return of the repressed"?

I suppose that is possible, but something more profuse or copious is imagined here. For what these displaced religious contents anticipate is not the romantic return to a traditional religious worldview, but rather the unexpected upheaval of the conventional conceptual terrain.[20] This critical dislocation is first glimpsed by recognizing the contingencies that mark the post-religious situation, then extricating from such contingency the prospect of thinking against the inertness of the whole.[21] In this fashion, the displaced fragments of religion furnish an "*Ausgang*," "exit," or "escape"[22] that simultaneously throws the reigning stasis into doubt. This subversive dynamic is curiously doubled, moreover, by the fact that such fragments of religion disrupt *as religious*: a real "*Ausgang*," after all, cannot be forged by tired signifiers that merely serve to remind. In order for the fragments to incise the non-religious in a truly critical way, the density of their religious shape and meaning cannot be overlooked nor explained away.

Now, this is not a statement of faith but a critical-theoretic observation with consequences for the discipline—

First, the constructive function of religious language *as* religious must be accented. This assignment, I believe, cannot be adequately explored by explaining religious terms as veiled signifiers of a more basic, exclusively human reality—regardless of whether that exclusivity is rendered in natural, scientific, psychological, sociological, or philosophical terms.[23] No, religious language involves more than saying something obvious about the world in less-than-obvious terms. Without dismissing the consideration of religious language as such, a more perceptive approach might ask "why" and "when" religious terms seem to be called into play. There are some types of human experience and knowledge, for example, that reflexively evoke religious terms as their point of explanation, justification, and conceptual fitness. Here religious terms arise, charge ahead, and assert themselves as vital for discernment. This view is by no means inspired by some hidden distress over the depreciation of dogma, but rather by the impoverishment of the kind, range, and depth of vocabulary needed to process the complex life. This does not mean that the range and weight of religious terms won't change over time—indeed, they will and must. The economy of religious language has its own circulation that permits different degrees of purchase at different points in time. *However, purchase there is.* We witness its arousal in various discourses, most notable the ethical, though this is hardly iron clad: poetic discourse and fictional narrative also come to mind.[24] What all this indicates, I hold, is that the reference, intimations, and imaginative qualities of religious terms cannot be repudiated as religious if the religious or spiritual character of such linguistic expressions is deemed indispensable for an increase in critical understanding. Such "epistemic gain,"[25] to call up Charles Taylor's phrase, contends that religious terms hold as religious if they are judged integral to a genuine increase in comprehension or clarity; an increase, moreover, that could not be had in another way at the particular time in question. So, if a term like "God" (to use a notorious example) is found to be positively key for creating a more thoughtful theory, then its explanatory power and value cannot be dismissed because it is religiously restricted, culturally confined, or personally bounded. If the term "God," in fact, comes off as crucial to the central meaning of things, it stays.

Second, it follows that this substance is something that requires interpretation via a "theological moment." It may seem odd to raise this prospect here. However, to unfold the critical contribution of religion for the enhanced differentiation of critical theory entails reflection on things theological. It does so because the substance carried by the fragments of religion in a post-religious context needs to be displayed, fathomed, and assayed in order to be critically salient. However, its goal is not to rescue or redeem a fading life-form (i.e., the religious itself, or the Jewish or Christian traditions, or their various denominations or embodiments), but rather to bring to bear an obscured religious content with the potential for transgression. The "theological moment," then, is but "a moment," and hardly definitive of the whole. It represents a single operation of thought within a much larger, composite process, that simultaneously delves into and relativizes the portent of the theological. Nevertheless, there is a real theological dispensation regardless of its critical circumspection and fragmentary state. Some critical insights will require a theological turn.

New cultural imperialism or post-Enlightenment modesty?

It would be both materially and historically untrue to deny an abiding religiosity that remains culturally significant. Yet this admission does not automatically sanction a totally universal, trans-historical, cross-cultural paradigm for religious thought—critical or otherwise. What it does mean is that religious particularity intrudes, forming part of the critical mix of things. However, it is a mix and it is critical: no particularism can make a tenable cognitive or ethical claim to exhaust the meaning of things—at least not at the theoretical level of thought. What has to be struggled with is if and how the bestowal of the religious particular enriches critical-theoretic thought. Thus, the emergent claim is not for a critical theory that is somehow more rational, more critical, or more complete because it is now religious. *No, the religious augmentation and increase of critical theory is undertaken for the sake of devising a different, though equally challenging form of critical theory that is also religious. It therefore bears witness to the religious as conceptual resource for theoretical innovation.*

Clearly, this declaration cannot be advanced without cautious reserve. Nevertheless, it can be rightly suggested that anything less than a vigilant, critical testing of diffuse but enduring religious contents would constitute a failure of thought.

Essays in Contemporary Religious Thought

It is with this challenge in mind that I advance the following "essays in contemporary religious thought" by charting the movement "from critical theology to a critical theory of religious insight."

To start things off, "From Postmodernity to Postorthodoxy, Or Charles

Davis and the Contemporary Context of Christian Thought" endeavours to outline a form of critical Christian thinking in relation to emerging types of postmodern culture and theological thought. By examining the affirmative, neo-conservative, and critical expressions of postmodernity in relation to constructive postmodern theology, deconstructive a/theology, and Other-directed theology, this study reveals the difficult construction of a contemporary theological thinking that is sufficiently critical on the one hand, while remaining tied to particular religious sources of insight, on the other. It is in response to this dilemma that I advance the work of Charles Davis as "postorthodox." Specifically, Davis' critique of religious orthodoxy—understood as a pre-modern essentialism impeding the development of an open faith—frees up the appropriation and application of religious tradition in relation to the postmodern search for new ways-of-being-in-the-world. While there is a tendency here to undermine the religious particularity demanded by the postmodern track, Davis' route still intimates how religious contents can creatively intersect to establish and extend the critical moment. In this case, then, critical postmodernism is completed as Christian postorthodoxy with its own potential course of development.

This development is further explored in the second essay, "Power/Knowledge and Liberation: Foucault as a Parabolic Thinker." Here I undertake another broad comparative analysis, this time between the philosophy of Michel Foucault and Liberation Theology. Aside from bringing two, quite desperate bodies of thought into creative dialogue, the contrast helps to throw into relief a facet of Foucault's work that remains vital to the remaining essays in this volume: namely, "transgressive transformation." As presented here, transgressive transformation constitutes the parabolic effect of critically retrieving "subjugated knowledges" that serve to challenge the unquestioned suppositions of the reigning normative order. In this way, retrieval alludes to critical change at the levels of thought and life. Now, aside from resonating with certain key themes in Liberation Theology—excavating the "dangerous memories" associated with "the preferential option for the poor," for example—transgressive transformation helps to make room for a religious thinking struggling with the character of the emancipatory interest in a postmodern context. While the dialogue with Liberation Theology contributes to an initial critical-religious interpretation of this interest, the discussion with Foucault extends that reading beyond its theological purview so as to reveal other possibilities. It is with these other possibilities that the remaining essays are concerned.

Thus the third essay, "The Moral-Existential Facet of Religious Studies Today," primarily announces the disciplinary framework that shapes the articulation of "a critical theory of religious insight"—namely, religious studies. While it is extremely difficult to sketch-out this framework in a decisive or even unambiguous way, I insist upon its difference for the project at hand. The essay contends that part of the purpose of religious studies is to facilitate the reflexive exploration of moral-existential frameworks of religious meaning in view of contemporary socio-cultural tensions, problems, and contradictions. Arguing now for a non-theological view of religious studies, it holds that it is capable of examining issues of religious truth, value, and purpose, though quite differently from theology. The first part of the study takes up the moral-existential facet of religious studies in relation to the modern fear of meaninglessness as a socio-cultural motivation for analysing sources of religious insight. To do so thoughtfully yet non-theologically, however, requires a new mode of critical deliberation which is expropriated from the work of Michel Foucault in part two. While the examination of Foucault's thought here is brief, the role and contribution of his philosophy are absolutely pivotal for this essay and beyond. Returning to the notion of "transgressive transformation," the paper pushes for a more creative, more speculative approach to criticism that is germane to the moral-existential facet of religious studies. By way of demonstrating the value of this critical design, part three sets out to untangle the postmodern contingencies motivating Jürgen Habermas' peculiar assessment of religious life and thought. For Habermas, the religious serves to keep postmodern philosophy at bay—a tactic that rebounds to betray his own want of a religiously informed social ethic. In order to meet that want, the final part of the essay presents a reflection on Emmanuel Levinas' unique view of the religio-ethical as that which transgressively transforms Habermas' position. On the other side of that transformation opens up the prospect of further work on the moral-existential facet of religious studies today as a critical theory of religious insight.

Following this general proposal, the fourth essay, "Fragments of Religion: An Exercise in Critical Post-Religious Thought" lays bear the socio-cultural grounding for a critical theory informed by religious ideas, themes, terms, and expressions. In this instance, the critical potential of religion is circumscribed by the post-religious situation that encourages the fragmentation and spread of religious contents into non-religious forms of thought. Part one of the essay explores this contemporary phenomenon in relation to the study of religion and modern historical, subjective, and artistic sensibilities. While this analysis leads to certain complexities for the role and function of religious thought today, I argue it is precisely within such a variegated context that critical religious thought belongs. The often unexpected juxtaposition of the religious and the non-religious generates new openings that serve to illuminate untried theoretical possibilities. In an effort to confirm this critical potential, part two takes up an examination of Albert Camus' exclusivist humanist view of rebellion. However, closer inspection reveals a vital religious fragment within Camus' presentation that presses for cultivation and expansion. Such a move on the part of the critical religious thinker, however, does not suggest that Camus' understanding of rebellion is ultimately religious or theological. Rather, I argue that such wayward religious fragments simply provide an important opportunity to extend thought (both religious and non-religious) in a new direction—here, beyond an exclusivist humanism. To be sure, this extension undoubtedly has consequences for the nature and character of religious thought in itself. For one, it implies the prospect of supporting rebellion, at least as a basic idea and ethic. However, that is not the closing point of the paper. It ends, rather, by emphasizing the various ways in which critical thought can be shaped in substantive religious terms. This cannot be ignored.

That it is not ignored is verified by the culminating essay of the volume, "A Critical Theory of Religious Insight." Here the structural, conceptual, and ethical components of the project are exposed and explained. This essay begins and ends with the question: "what is the meaning and purpose of religious thought today?" In response to this query, this article outlines the critical significance of the socio-cultural fragmentation of contemporary religious thought by: first, reclaiming an ethical moment within the critical theory of Max Horkheimer; second, justifying the significance of that moment by expanding the understanding of morality as explained by Charles Taylor; and third, cultivating its religio-ethical content in relation to Emmanuel Levinas' understanding of God as an ethical force that interrupts, subverts, and throws into question. Horkheimer's early version of critical theory is singled out as key to the development of a critical religious thinking since his work admits a significant (and fascinating) moral impulse that the other critical theorists from the Frankfurt School—including its second generation—tend to neglect. Charles Taylor's investigations of morality and moral thought further encourages a critical appropriation of the moral impulse at work within Horkheimer's early critical theory while necessarily guiding it beyond the limits set by secular critical theory. One of those directions is the religio-ethical. Through the highly original and unusual work of Levinas, a twined critical dynamic and religious content cuts through all secular hesitation. It is this juxtaposition of themes and figures, then, that points toward a critical theory informed by religious insights. What it represents—and what all the essays in this volume essentially intend—is an untried form of critical theory whose religio-ethical cast and substance contributes to the venture of contemporary thinking by working with the fragility of religious thought today.

Notes

1. Michel Foucault, "The Masked Philosopher," trans. Robert Hurley and others, in *Ethics: Subjectivity and Truth*, vol. 1 of *The Essential Works of Michel Foucault, 1954–1984*, ed. Paul Rabinow (New York: The New Press, 1997), 327.
2. For an interesting analysis of this explosion see Terry Eagleton, *The Significance of Theory* (Oxford: Basil Blackwell, 1990), 24–38.
3. Craig Calhoun, *Critical Social Theory: Culture, History, and the Challenge of Difference* (Oxford: Blackwell, 1995), 10, 88.
4. Marc P. Lalonde, *Critical Theology and the Challenge of Jürgen Habermas: Toward a Critical Theory of Religious Insight* (New York: Peter Lang, 1999).
5. See J.B. Metz, *Faith in History and Society: Toward a Practical Fundamental Theology*, trans. David Smith (New York: Crossroad, 1980), and Helmult Peukert, *Science, Action, and Fundamental Theology: Toward a Theology of Communicative Action*, trans. James Bohman (Cambridge, Mass.: MIT Press, 1986).
6. See Charles Davis, *Theology and Political Society* (Cambridge: Cambridge University Press, 1980); Alfredo Fierro, *The Militant Gospel: A Critical Introduction of Political Theologies*, trans. John Drury (Maryknoll, NY: Orbis Books, 1977); and Alistar Kee, *Marx and the Failure of Liberation Theology* (London: SCM Press, 1990).
7. On this point see Dennis P. McCann's critique of Liberation Theology in *Christian Realism and Liberation Theology: Practical Theologies in Creative Conflict* (Maryknoll, NY: Orbis Books, 1981).
8. Rudolf Siebert seems to me to be one of the worst offenders along these lines. See his books, *The Critical Theory of Religion: The Frankfurt School. From Universal Pragmatic to Political Theology* (New York: Mouton, 1985), and *From Critical Theory to Communicative Political Theology: Universal Solidarity* (New York: Peter Lang, 1989). However, the basic claim holds for most theologians endeavouring to use critical theory to construct a contemporary form of Christian thought with argumentative weight.
9. Douglas John Hall, *The End of Christendom and the Future of Christianity* (Eugene, Oregon: Wipf and Stock Publishers, 1997), 51.
10. See Metz, *Faith in History and Society*, 32–48.
11. See Thomas J. J. Altizer and William Hamilton, *Radical Theology and the Death of God* (New York: The Bobbs-Merrill Company, 1966). In Mark C. Taylor's essay, "Postmodern

Times," in *The Otherness of God*, ed. Orrin F. Summerell (Charlottesville: University Press of Virginia, 1998), the author clearly situates death of God theology in relation to developments in postmodern culture and thought (183).
12. See Mark C. Taylor, *Erring: A Postmodern A/Theology* (Chicago: University of Chicago Press, 1984).
13. Also see the introduction to Marc P. Lalonde ed., *The Promise of Critical Theology: Essays in Honour of Charles Davis* (Waterloo, Ontario: Wilfrid Laurier University Press, 1995), 1–22.
14. Charles Taylor, *Sources of the Self: The Making of the Modern Identity* (Cambridge, Mass.: Harvard University Press, 1989), 3–5.
15. The phrase is of course Thomas Nagel's. See his book *The View From Nowhere* (New York: Oxford University Press, 1986).
16. See, for example, Max Horkheimer, "Thoughts on Religion," in *Critical Theory: Selected Essays*, trans. Matthew J. O'Connell and others (New York: Continuum, 1972); and Jürgen Habermas, "Metaphysics After Kant," in *Postmetaphysical Thinking: Philosophical Essays*, trans. William Mark Hohengarten (Cambridge, Mass.: MIT Press, 1992).
17. For a complex example of this approach to things see John Milbank, *Theology and Social Theory: Beyond Secular Reason* (Oxford: Basil Blackwell, 1990). Also see the writings of the so-called "radical orthodox" group in John Milbank, Catherine Pickstock, and Graham Ward eds., *Radical Orthodoxy: A New Theology* (London: Routledge, 1999). For a more critical perspective see Gavin Hyman, *The Predicament of Postmodern Theology: Radical Orthodoxy or Textual Nihilism?* (Louisville: Westminster John Knox Press, 2001).
18. These themes come to the fore in the work of Max Horkheimer as analyzed in the final essay, "A Critical Theory of Religious Insight." However, similar concerns also surface, in one form or another, in the work of Adorno and Habermas, though all in very different ways.
19. See for example Michel Despland's book *Reading an Erased Code: Romantic Religion and Literary Aesthetics in France* (Toronto: University of Toronto Press, 1994), which details the migration of religious ideas into a new Romantic aesthetic and philosophical form of argument.
20. Gilles Deleuze, "Nomad Thought," in *The New Nietzsche*, ed. David B. Allison (Cambridge, Mass.: MIT Press, 1985), 144.
21. Michel Foucault, "What is Enlightenment?" trans. Robert Hurley and others, in *Ethics: Subjectivity and Truth*, vol. 1 of *The Essential Works of Michel Foucault, 1954–1984*, ed. Paul Rabinow (New York: The New Press, 1997), 315–316.
22. Ibid., 305.
23. See my critique of Albert Camus' "exclusive humanism" in the fourth essay, "Fragments of Religion: An Exercise in Critical Post-Religious Thought."
24. See the essays and interviews by Paul Ricoeur in *A Ricoeur Reader: Reflection and Imagination*, ed. Mario J. Valdés (Toronto: University of Toronto Press, 1991), especially "Poetry and Possibility," 448–462.
25. Taylor, *Sources of the Self*, 71–73.

Essay One

From Postmodernity to Postorthodoxy, Or Charles Davis and the Contemporary Context of Christian Thought

IN THEIR introduction to the volume *Paradigm Change in Theology: A Symposium for the Future*, editors Hans Küng and David Tracy characterize the present cultural and theological situation as a "time of troubles." It is a "postmodern time," they say, in which rational and metaphysical certainties have crashed upon the horrors of Auschwitz and Hiroshima; a time where the "hegemony" of modern western civilization has been subverted by the challenge of cultural and religious pluralism; a time where the "otherness" of such pluralism confronts individual consciousness with its lack of a secure identity. "How does this affect the proclamation?" ask Küng and Tracy, and "How can theology be 'contemporary,' yet true to its identity?"[1]

These enduring questions go to the heart of a modern Christian thinking that appears to suddenly find itself in drastically altered circumstances. The dilemma seems fixed: the proclamation, in order to be "true," must be true "now" if it is to be true at all. Yet what if this "now" is plainly inhospitable or hostile to the proclamation as such? Can it survive? Without surprise, this quandary almost never concludes in real despair. It rather ends as an opportunity to re-assert the triumph of the Spirit. But what are we to make, then, of our so-called "time of troubles" when an untroubled solution is anticipated from the start? A lack of critical vigilance.

Note—this objection is not a roundabout way of declaring the exhaustion of Christian (or Jewish, or Buddhist) thought—Auschwitz and Hiroshima require their religious redress too. To attain this, a *critical* form of contemporary religious thought demands clarification. In the offing here is an open-ended, exploratory type of Christian thinking that resonates with the postmodern cultural situation. Its rudimentary configuration is pursued via an analysis of two theological positions that evince support for the critical moment in contemporary culture: an assortment of "postmodern theologies," on the one hand, and the "postorthodox"[2] deliberations of Charles Davis, on the other. What their comparison shows is that the diverse forms of postmodern theology are insufficiently critical in relation to postmodern thought and culture, while Davis' postorthodoxy portends a type of Christian reflection that lays the ground for a more rigorous form of critical religious thought.

The Postmodern Cultural Situation

Considered historically, "postmodernity" involves three major cultural trends: (i) an affirmative postmodernism, (ii) a neoconservative postmodernism, and (iii) an alternative or critical postmodernism.[3]

The first trend emerges in North America after the disintegration of the counter-culture ethos of the 1960s. Its collapse, observes Andreas Huyssen, ushers in an ad hoc approach to cultural expression, "characterized ... by an ever wider dispersal and dissemination of artistic practices all working out of the ruins of the modernist edifice, raiding it for ideas, plundering its vocabulary and supplementing it with randomly chosen images and motifs from pre-modern and non-modern cultures as well as from contemporary mass culture."[4] This description underlines the ruin of the high art/low art dichotomy. In its place arises a "post-modern pastiche" which, as Fredric Jameson explains, constitutes a form of "blank parody."[5] The purpose of parody usually is to provide satirical comment on particular modes of cultural expression. It remains bound to some kind of normative tradition, if only to mock its eccentricities. Postmodern pastiche is mimicry devoid of norm or intent. For Jameson, this barren practice betrays a repercussion of the dissolved doctrine of high modernist style which endeavours to create something original. With its marginalization, we procure "a world in which stylistic innovation is no longer possible, [and] all that is left is to imitate *dead styles...*"[6]

Of utmost importance is the manner in which this aesthetic eclecticism signifies the dehistoricization of contemporary culture. Jameson cites the popularization of the "nostalgia" film as an example of this phenomenon. He contends it is not an attempt to clarify the relationship between the past and the present, but advances a *style of filming* which evokes a vague sense of "pastness" through the indiscriminate display of antiquated aesthetic objects and fashions.[7] This retreat into nostalgia diverts attention away from the present socio-political conditions, while the past is portrayed as shifting fads in commercial merchandise. Jameson therefore sees an ideological link between "*la mode rétro*" and the economic interests of the consumerist society.[8]

Affirmative postmodernism thus "affirms" the consumerist ethos by indiscriminately imaging the present as the historicity of changing fashion.

The dehistoricization of culture sets the stage for the second postmodern trend, neoconservatism. It appears to be reacting to affirmative postmodernism, claiming that the subversion of traditional quality, value, and identity contributes to a moral and economic crisis within the western world.[9] Jürgen Habermas contends that the neoconservative judges cultural change as detrimental to the "moral basis" which supports a "purposive, rational conduct of life."[10] This conduct is viewed as absolutely vital for preserving western economic prosperity and affluence. To avoid further decay, one must impede moral degeneration by reinstituting the conventional values and social roles common to the lifeworld of the 1950s. Yet the disorientation of moral sensibility in western society is not the result of cultural innovation but an effect of the very prosperity and affluence which the neoconservative desires to protect. Habermas writes: "The neoconservatives confuse cause and effect. In place of the economic and administrative imperatives, the so-called objective constraints that are monetarizing and bureaucratizing more and more domains of life and increasingly transforming relationships into commodities and objects of administration—in place of these true sources of social crises the neoconservatives put the spectre of a subversively degenerate culture."[11]

Neoconservative postmodernism thus ironically constitutes a reactionary response to a cultural-economic situation fostered itself by the interests of the neoconservative.

Given the character of both affirmative and neoconservative postmodernism, the development of a critical perspective is one of the major challenges facing western culture today. Huyssen, for one, contends this challenge is being met by a critical postmodernism. This last trend involves the search for alternative traditions and histories which may establish communal identity while endorsing the transformation of modern life. Critical postmodernism "manifests itself in the concern with cultural formations not dominated by logocentric and technocratic thought, in the decentering of...traditional notions of identity, in the search for women's history, in the rejection of centralism, mainstreams, and melting pots of all kinds, and in the great value put on difference and otherness."[12] Critical leverage is provided by the notion of alterity. It compels a dialectical tension between tradition and innovation which neither rejects the value of tradition, nor ignores the summons for change.[13] Critical postmodernism is both "critical" and "postmodern" because its accent on "otherness"—i.e., those subjugated features of tradition and human experience concealed by normative explanations of how things "truly" are—exposes the oppressive ramifications of any rigid traditionalism that ignores its own plurality as well as debunking a misplaced faith in a ceaseless modernization that inherently negates all past forms of life. On the far side of this dialectic stands the search for particular postmodern identities with real substance.

Alternative postmodernism thus concerns the critical reconstruction of a tradition so that it points to a credible way of living beyond modern patterns of life and thought.

Varieties of Postmodern Theology

Postmodern Christian thought must be assessed in view of this historico-cultural context.

An appropriate place to begin is with the book *Varieties of Postmodern Theology*. Its most conspicuous facet is the juxtaposition of what David Ray Griffin calls "eliminative postmodern theology," i.e., those theologies inspired by Derridean deconstruction, and Griffin's own position which he describes as a "constructive postmodern theology."

Griffin's analysis of eliminative postmodernism focuses on Mark C. Taylor's work *Erring: A Postmodern A/Theology*. He acknowledges that Taylor's critique of modern domination *is* inspired by a moral concern to eradicate oppression.[14] "The master who *needs* to be master," writes Taylor, "is no master at all. The historical agent's struggle for mastery and quest for domination indicate irrepressible deficiency by revealing the *need* to appropriate otherness."[15] Still, Griffin criticizes eliminative postmodernism as that which "overcomes the modern worldview through an anti-worldview: it deconstructs or eliminates the ingredients necessary for a worldview, such as God, self, purpose, meaning, a real world, and truth as correspondence."[16] The erasure of traditional modes of thought and truth championed by Taylor's deconstructive strategy undermines the theoretical basis for a postmodern religious criticism.[17] It therefore appears to exhibit a performative contradiction: while the poststructuralist disclosure of modern forms of domination evokes an emancipatory interest, its theoretical suppositions seem to thwart the significance of that interest by negating the conceptual tools necessary for overcoming domination as such.[18]

In response to this dilemma, Griffin proposes a positive postmodern worldview anchored in a revision of modern ideas and traditional concepts.[19] Griffin's position appears to conform to a critical postmodernism, manoeuvring, as it does, between tradition and innovation. However, he radically reduces the risk of such revision by grounding his alternative in an epistemological privilege that not only tries to outstrip any performative contradiction, but seeks to cut straight through the cultural and theological ambiguity created by his reconstructive project.

> According to revisionary postmodernism…some universally acknowledged facts are to be found. They are acknowledged in practice by everyone, even if they are denied verbally. They are acknowledged in what I call *hard-core common sense notions*.…A truly (hard-core) common sense notion is one that *cannot be denied without contradicting one's own practice*…Acting with the purpose of inducing others to believe that there is no such thing as causal influence and purposive activity [as does eliminative postmodernism] is…self-contradictory.[20]

What are the weaknesses of this petition for "hard-core" common sense notions? While one may wish to affirm a theoretical-practical contiguity, a practical contradiction does not automatically terminate the theoretical insight. And even if one agrees that eliminative postmodernism is theoretically doubtful given its practice, does this problem warrant the inviolable epistemology advocated by Griffin? I do not think that it does. The conception of "hard-core common sense notions" suggests a neoconservative response to the cultural, and now, theological confusion initiated by the postmodern critique of universal meaning. The challenge to intellectual and religious certitude engendered by that critique compels compensation through elementary ideas such as "common sense." However, simplicity cannot be equated with either justice or truth.[21] To insist that "universally acknowledged facts" are recognized "by everyone, even if they are denied verbally," imposes a "Truth" upon the self-understanding of the "other," despite all objections to the contrary. In effect, Griffin's proposal does not overcome eliminative postmodernism, but confirms its diagnosis.

Rather than trying to illustrate how the mode of argumentation in eliminative postmodernism reveals a practical reliance on an implicit universality or "Truth," it is perhaps more profitable to examine its peculiar practice. Deconstruction is a strategy of reading, writing, and thinking which unmasks a pervasive linguistic instability, splintering "rational" coherence for the sake of an alterity that cannot be eclipsed.[22] Deconstruction is more than a process, however. It hinges on specific themes and images which are necessary to appreciate it as a theoretical practice that defends "otherness."[23] This defence reveals more than a performative contradiction. Observe Taylor's choice of the following passage from Derrida in support of a/theology:

> "This signifier of little, this discourse that doesn't amount to much, is, like all ghosts: errant. It rolls...like someone who has lost his way,...but also like someone who has lost his rights, an outlaw, a pervert, a bad seed, a vagrant, a bum. Wandering the streets, he doesn't even know who he is, what his identity—if he has one—might be, what his name is, what his father's name is...Uprooted, anonymous, unattached to any house or country, this almost insignificant signifier is at everyone's disposal..."[24]

Depicting the free-floating signifier as a homeless person for its rhetorical effectiveness serves to obscure the historical actuality of the street person. The celebration of homelessness and facelessness as a way to emphasize the value of transgression, undercuts the notable insight that might accrue from the critique of the possessive western identity. In this light, Taylor's a/theology seems to support an affirmative postmodernism and its function within consumerist society: any thing—or any body—can be reified.

A more penetrating expression of postmodern theology is provided by Edith Wyschogrod's essay, "Man-Made Mass Death: Shifting Concepts of Community." The author claims that the unprecedented nature of our age of mass death demands the search for unprecedented communities.[25] Wyschogrod contends that there are definite aspects of poststructuralist thought which can assist us in this search by intimating the kinds of expressions such communities may take on. She also records her virtual reliance upon this philosophy: "Although social existence, even community, is considered in ... [postmodern] literature, nowhere is there a focus upon community that begins with our ordinary understanding of the word, so I am compelled to draw out the implications of this body of work as it bears on the meaning of community."[26] This "drawing out of the implications" reveals more than asymmetric understandings of community. Wyschogrod merges analyses of Lyotard's "differend" with Levinas' religio-ethical conception of the "Other,"[27] while Blanchot's "unavowable community" as an "excess in the context of erotic relations" is interpreted as "the desire for the preservation of human existence in the face of the possible extinction of humankind. This impulse flows...from the moral subject, that dimension of the subject in which the Other takes precedence over the self."[28] The emphasis on alterity certainly helps to unmask the modern ideology of "sameness" which stands behind the age of mass death.[29] In opposition to this age, Wyschogrod explores a social ethic through which communities band together in the name of the irreducible Other. However, she expounds this ethic without critically addressing the need to supplement postmodern philosophy with a religio-ethical content. The issue that surfaces concerns the reason for a theological appropriation of postmodern thought in the first place. For if it is religion that authenticates the critical weight of Wyschogrod's deliberation, then exactly what does postmodern philosophy contribute to her presentation?

Critical postmodernism gains its significance from the notion of alterity that frees up the search for alternative but positive formulations of individual and communal identity. The theological application of this critical category, however, reveals the difficulty of trying to join its negative function with its positive intention. Taylor's critique of the possessive western identity, for instance, nicely illustrates the emancipatory potential of alterity as such, yet it exalts negativity in a brutal fashion. Griffin's attempt to resolve this obstacle reinstitutes a triumphant universal "Truth" as the only way to ground a positive expression of postmodernity. However, this option fails to seriously confront the immanent critical force of alterity.

Given this impasse, Wyschogrod's approach appears to be a successful synthesis. Her argument is rooted in the critical function of alterity as an ethic of social solidarity against the violent reduction and oppression of "otherness." Thus, *pace* Griffin, Wyschogrod recapitulates the critical rigour of alterity; and *pace* Taylor, she consolidates the emancipatory purpose of alterity in a contemporary context. Yet her presentation makes clear that the ethical force of alterity as a positive social ethic is underwritten by religious sources of insight. The critical need to supplement postmodern thought with a religious content indicates that it is *not* postmodern philosophy which permits the creation of a critical postmodern religious thinking, but rather that it is religious thought that augments the prospect of a critical postmodernism.[30]

Postorthodox Religious Thought

That prospect receives one of its finest expressions as a "postorthodox" form of Christian thought.

In *What is Living, What is Dead in Christianity Today?* Charles Davis describes contemporary culture oscillating between metaphysics and nihilism: a vacillation that corresponds to the neoconservative and affirmative trends in postmodernity respectively. The metaphysical extreme responds to the transitory nature of historical reality by positing eternal norms that guide human knowledge and judgement. This attitude disparages cultural change and pluralism, and advances an ideal objective for all cultural expression. On the other hand, contemporary experience includes a technocratic nihilism. By this Davis is referring to the trivialization of substantial meaning and value which results from the formal rationality common to the totally administered society. Both trends abandon history by fostering a quasi-certitude in the face of life's contingencies. Their promise of providing a final meaning, however, is unconvincing because a metaphysical embodiment of truth can no longer grasp the modern imagination as true, while technocratic nihilism frustrates the search for substantial values and ends.[31]

How should the Christian react to this state of affairs? Davis submits that the path between metaphysics and nihilism requires Christians to select facets of their religious heritage pertinent to their ongoing existence.[32] Davis is not advocating the creation of a specifically "postmodern theology," but arguing for an understanding of Christian faith which illuminates how it is capable of responding to the exigencies of the current era while rooting itself in tradition. As such, this option intimates how a religious moment arises within critical postmodernism as a postorthodoxy.

Davis' reconstruction begins by recognizing the fluidity and flexibility of the Christian symbol system that follows from the poetic character of religious language and narrative. Religious symbols "are polysemous," remarks Davis, "carrying a plurality of meanings, not merely successively but simultaneously."[33] Religious language and symbol cannot literally constitute intellectual or political positions. As polysemous *they do not provide the kind of certitude longed for by both metaphysics and nihilism.* Nevertheless, Davis realizes that the cultural embodiment and expression of religious meaning cannot be bypassed without either reducing this meaning to an intellectualism, and thereby contributing to an epistemology that functions as a metaphysics (e.g., Griffin's constructive postmodernism), or denying that such symbols have any meaning whatsoever, thereby contributing to the forces of modern nihilism (e.g., Taylor's a/theology). If contemporary religious thought is to avoid both extremes, this means that it must involve itself "in a constant process of deconstruction and reconstruction as the implications of its own praxis in ever-new situations transforms its theoretical self-understanding."[34]

The primary effect of this "constant process" is evinced by Davis' critique of religious orthodoxy. Here the conception of tradition is identified with adherence to propositions in the form of dogmatic truths accepted on the basis of authority:

> Religion when maintained as an orthodoxy claims a permanent self-identity remaining

unscathed by social and practical changes. It invokes some purely theoretical centre of reference to serve in an abstract speculative way as a norm of identity…The presupposition of orthodoxy is the contemplative conception of knowledge, according to which knowledge is the result of the disinterested viewing of reality by individuals.[35]

Orthodoxy for Davis is the result of a synthesis of *mythos* and *logos*. This combination establishes an "ontotheology" which Davis defines as the "attempt to translate the content of the Christian myth into the theoretical concepts and statements of metaphysical philosophy."[36] The difficulty with this translation is its effort to maintain the certitude appropriate to myth and religious narrative (i.e., the trust which arises when the narrative constitutes the integral framework of practical experience) for a mode of knowledge which, *in principle*, does not allow for such an existential conviction. "Once one has left myth and entered into conceptual analysis and carefully measured rational affirmations," writes Davis, "one is confined to the limited, tentative results of theoretical reflection, results always subject to further development, reformulation, and revision."[37] The orthodox assertion of a "permanent Christian self-identity" is based upon a theoretical orientation that does not allow for such a claim.

There is more involved in the critique of orthodoxy than showing up a theoretical contradiction. Davis contends that the ontotheological misappropriation of the certitude of myth displaces the experiential basis for such a conviction with the pseudo-certitude of dogma that impedes the dynamic practice of faith. It does so because the "Christian faith is a transforming principle, not a body of objective knowledge."[38] What a transforming faith provides is "a basic assurance through which we can live with love and trust in the midst of the inescapable negativities and unanswered questions of human existence."[39] As Davis elaborates:

> The absoluteness of faith is the absoluteness of total demand and total response in an experience of *unrestricted love* in relation to hidden transcendence or mystery. Faith is the drive toward transcendence, the thrust of human beings out and beyond themselves, out of and beyond all the limited orders and human certainties under which they live, in an attempt to open themselves to the totality of existence and reach unlimited reality and ultimate value.[40]

This quotation reveals the core of Davis' postorthodoxy: it is love which is foundational for Christian existence in its social, cultural and political expressions, and not knowledge. It is love that substantiates the basic assurance of faith, and which propels the Christian practices which forms its traditions.

If, however, the dynamic of unrestricted love appears to undercut all particular expressions of that love, what positive tradition could ever develop? This problem comes to the fore in Davis' tendency to devalue religious particularism via his critique of religious exclusivity.[41] As he interprets the issue, "the scandal of particularity, namely, the once-for-all character of Christian revelation,…necessarily implies that other religions purvey only partial truth, calling for correction and completion by the fullness of Christian revelation."[42] The question that suggests itself here is whether, and to what degree, such a self-understanding is dependent on an exclusive, or even triumphant presentation of one's religious tradition in order to maintain itself as tradition? My response is that religious exclusivity and religious particularism are not the same thing, and Davis' critique of religious orthodoxy contributes to a clarification of their difference.

Religious particularism results from the cultural, social, and political mediation of the unrestricted love *as part of* its movement as a totality. As Emil Fackenheim once noted, "If God is ever present *in history*, this is not a presence-in-general but rather a presence to particular men in particular situations."[43] The result is a particular witness that gives rise to distinctive theistic traditions. In theological terms, each tradition may be said to give voice to the mystery of God's hidden presence. Hidden, because the infinite God cannot fully disclose itself through the finite: yet present, because infinitely capable of finite mediation.[44]

The mediated experience of God as unrestricted love should *not* be confused with an exclusive or absolutist notion of religious truth. This confusion arises when the process of mediation is truncated, and one particular revelation of the hidden presence of God is accepted as a full disclosure of the divine and claims to overcome the confines of God's hiddenness. In this way, the particular is identified as an ontic manifestation of God and functions as a stable criterion for judgements of "Truth."[45] However, in order for the particular to be particular, it cannot at the same time be exclusive without supplanting the transcendent which marks the particular as a finite nodal point for the divine-human encounter. The conditions for the possibility of the particular as mediator of the divine love are also the conditions for the impossibility of an absolutization of the particular as an orthodoxy. Orthodoxy is the temptation of the particular not its fulfilment. Its fulfilment resides in being a communicator for that which is larger than itself: the unrestricted love.

A postorthodox tradition is therefore a *fragile* but supple vehicle for the fragments of divine love that reach out to us, from time to time, through the particular. God's love, and the turning of that love toward the world, implores a human *re-turning* by actively taking up this love in our historical day-to-day lives. This praxis, embodied as tradition, releases the fragments of divine love from their hiddenness by mobilizing that love in accord with its own unrestricted movement. This requires a radical openness to the opportunities for love which cannot be managed as if it were a factory product. Love is unpredictable which is why the divine love undermines "the limited orders and human certitudes under which we live."[46] But this transformative force is hardly automatic. *For love is not something that can grow by itself: it lives insofar that it occurs between two lovers.*[47]

Conclusion

Critical postmodernism entails the appropriation and reconstruction of particular ethical, social, and religious orientations capable of respecting, and learning from, the plurality of cultural difference and otherness available within the secular milieu. The full implication of this context for the development of critical postmodern religious thought is not easy to discern. On the one hand, how does one truly differentiate between an emancipatory alterity and the eclectic alterity of affirmative postmodernism and, on the other hand, between the critical reconstruction of tradition and a neoconservative reaction?

The analysis of postmodern theology indicates that the particularism demanded by critical postmodernism necessitates the adoption of a specific tradition which can substantiate the emancipatory values advocated by this postmodern trend. Taylor's neglect of this factor manifests itself as a celebration of negativity, while Wyschogrod uncritically supplements her postmodern sources with religious themes in order to avoid the same conclusion. Yet Griffin's effort to establish the particularity of a postmodern religious worldview in an epistemology of "common sense" tends to occlude otherness, and, in the end, supports the neoconservative trend. One central question which the critical postmodern religious thinker must address is whether it is possible to establish the particularity required by a critical postmodernism while eluding both the nihilistic consequences of affirmative postmodernism and the metaphysical claims of neoconservatism?

At this juncture, Davis' postorthodoxy comes to the fore as an authentic expression of critical postmodern Christian thought. His assertion that love is foundational for Christian existence rather than knowledge points toward a presentation of religious particularity which necessarily rejects the trivialization of substantial value represented by affirmative postmodernism, and the moral-intellectual certitude longed for by the neoconservative. This position is established by a deconstruction of religious orthodoxy in order to retrieve the practical function and dynamic of the Christian narrative as the positive framework through which to critically respond to the various challenges of the contemporary situation. Though a postorthodox approach to the Christian tradition may seem to threaten the particularity that supports the uniqueness of its faith, "Once the transcendence of Christian experience has been recognized," writes Davis, "the indispensable function of tradition…re-emerges, even after the rejection of a doctrinalized form of tradition…"[48]

Notes

1. Hans Küng and David Tracy eds., *Paradigm Change in Theology: A Symposium for the Future* (New York: Crossroad, 1989), xv.
2. By the term "postorthodox" I intend a type of theology that emerges on the far side of religious authoritarian structures of life and thought. It is meant to function as an introductory designation of Davis' overall position. However, it is a temporary designation since it fails to do justice to the real depth of his theological vision that is explored in the final section of this essay. Nevertheless, "postorthodoxy" does serve as an initial marker of Davis' central argument and descriptively situates his work within the contemporary theological and philosophical context. But in the final analysis, Davis' theology points beyond postorthodoxy to a more particularistic Christian expression that has yet to be fully articulated either by Davis or his expositors.
3. Andreas Huyssen, *After the Great Divide: Modernism, Mass Culture, Postmodernism* (Bloomington: Indiana University Press, 1986), 160–221.
4. Ibid., 196.
5. Fredric Jameson, "Postmodernism and Consumer Society," in *The Anti-Aesthetic: Essays on Postmodern Culture*, ed. Hal Foster (Port Townsend, Washington: Bay Press, 1983), 114.
6. Ibid., 115. Italics added. Also see Fredric Jameson, *Postmodernism, Or, The Cultural Logic of Late Capitalism* (Durham : Duke University Press, 1991), 17–18.
7. Jameson, "Postmodernism and Consumer Society," 116–117; *Postmodernism*, 19–20.
8. Jameson, "Postmodernism and Consumer Society," 125; *Postmodernism*, x–xxii, 55–66.
9. Huyssen, *After the Great Divide*, 204. Also see Russell A. Berman, *Modern Culture and Critical Theory: Art, Politics, and the Legacy of the Frankfurt School* (Madison, WI: University of Wisconsin Press, 1989), 43; Jürgen Habermas, *The New Conservatism: Cultural Criticism and the Historians' Debate*, trans. Shierry Weber Nicholson (Cambridge, Mass.: MIT Press, 1989), 23.
10. Jürgen Habermas, "Modernity—An Incomplete Project," in *The Anti-Aesthetic: Essays on*

      Postmodern Culture, ed. Hal Foster (Port Townsend, Washington: Bay Press, 1983), 6.
11. Habermas, *New Conservatism*, 44.
12. Huyssen, *After The Great Divide*, 172.
13. Ibid., 216.
14. David Ray Griffin, "Postmodern Theology and A/Theology: A Response to Mark C. Taylor," in David Ray Griffin, William A. Beardslee, and Joe Holland, *Varieties of Postmodern Theology* (Albany, NY: SUNY Press, 1989), 39.
15. Mark C. Taylor, *Erring: A Postmodern A/Theology* (Chicago: University of Chicago Press, 1984), 69.
16. David Ray Griffin, "Introduction to SUNY Series in Constructive Postmodern Thought," in Griffin, Beardslee, and Holland, *Varieties of Postmodern Theology*, xii.
17. Griffin, "Postmodern Theology and A/Theology," 39.
18. On the notion of a "performative contradiction" see the essays that deal with Foucault and Derrida in Jürgen Habermas, *The Philosophical Discourse of Modernity: Twelve Lectures*, trans. Frederick G. Lawrence (Cambridge, Mass.: MIT Press, 1987). Also see Charles Taylor, "Foucault on Freedom and Truth," in *Foucault: A Critical Reader*, ed. David Couzens Hoy (Oxford: Basil Blackwell, 1986); Sheldon S. Wolin, "On the Theory and Practice of Power," in *After Foucault: Humanistic Knowledge, Postmodern Challenges*, ed. Jonathan Arac (New Brunswick: Rutgers University Press, 1988); Nancy Fraser, "The French Derrideans: Politicizing Deconstruction or Deconstructing the Political?" in *Unruly Practices: Power Discourse and Gender in Contemporary Social Theory* (Minneapolis: University of Minnesota Press, 1989); Gregory Baum, "Theories of Post-Modernity," *The Ecumenist* 29 (1991): 4–12.
19. Griffin, "Introduction," xii.
20. Griffin, "Postmodern Theology and A/Theology," 40.
21. See Habermas, *New Conservatism*, 42–43.
22. See Christopher Norris, *Deconstruction: Theory and Practice* (London: Routledge, 1982).
23. See Kevin Hart, *The Trespass of the Sign: Deconstruction, Theology, and Philosophy* (Cambridge: Cambridge University Press, 1989), 64.
24. Taylor, *Erring*, 149.
25. Edith Wyschogrod, "Man-Made Mass Death: Shifting Concepts of Community," *Journal of the American Academy of Religion* 58 (1990): 167–168.
26. Ibid., 168.
27. Ibid., 171–172.
28. Ibid., 173.
29. Also see Zygmunt Bauman, *Modernity and the Holocaust* (Cambridge: Polity Press, 1989).
30. For a similar though far more complex thesis which yields a radically different conclusion than the one reached in this essay, see John Milbank, *Theology and Social Theory: Beyond Secular Reason* (Oxford: Basil Blackwell, 1990).
31. Charles Davis, *What is Living, What is Dead in Christianity Today? Breaking the Liberal-Conservative Deadlock* (San Francisco: Harper and Row, 1986), 1–6.
32. Ibid., 55.
33. Ibid., 5.

34. Ibid., 2.
35. Charles Davis, *Theology and Political Society* (Cambridge: Cambridge University Press, 1980), 130.
36. Davis, *What is Living?* 60.
37. Ibid., 109.
38. Ibid., 71.
39. Ibid., 68.
40. Ibid., 67. Italics added.
41. Ibid., 106–123.
42. Ibid., 107.
43. Emil Fackenheim, *God's Presence in History: Jewish Affirmations and Philosophical Reflections* (New York: Harper Torchbooks, 1972), 8.
44. Cf. Richard P. McBrien, *Catholicism: Study Edition* (San Francisco: Harper and Row, 1981), 232–234.
45. Ibid. It is for this reason that I choose to employ the term "mystery" rather than "incarnation" to envision the presence of God in history. Though the notion and doctrine of the "incarnation of God" is often equated with the "mystery of God," the two ideas admit some important differences. "God-as-mystery" underscores the dialectic of the divine presence and absence in history, while "the incarnation of God" implies God revealing *and* God revealed. As McBrien explains the incarnation of God's presence in history; "Christ always remains the supreme moment of revelation, both as process and as product, because in Christ alone God's self-communication totally transforms the mediator, so that the mediator and the mediated are one and the same. Christ is not only our 'go-between' with God. He is also 'very God of very God'…" (235) On the other hand, God-as-mystery suggests that "God remains at the same time veiled and unveiled. We cannot escape the realm of ambiguity" (234). Cf. Davis' critique of Karl Rahner's conception of transcendental revelation in *What is Living?* 57–59.
46. Davis, *What is Living?* 67.
47. Cf. Martin Buber, *I and Thou*, trans. Walter Kaufmann (New York: Charles Scribner's Sons, 1970), 66; *Between Man and Man*, trans. Ronald Gregor Smith (New York: Macmillan, 1965), 1–39.
48. Davis, *What is Living?* 80.

Essay Two

Power/Knowledge and Liberation: Foucault as a Parabolic Thinker

LET ME begin by posing a plain but complex question: "Why should the Christian liberation or political theologian struggle with the 'power/knowledge' configuration as formulated by the French philosopher Michel Foucault?" Charles Taylor's pointed characterization of Foucault's work proclaims that "the idea of a liberating truth is a profound illusion [for Foucault]. There is no truth that can be espoused, defended, rescued, against systems of power. On the contrary, each such system defines its own variant of truth. And there is no escape from power into freedom, for such systems of power are co-extensive with human society. We can only step from one to another."[1] Since emancipation from political oppression and injustice represents the quintessential criterion for an authentic liberation theology, its engagement of power/knowledge would appear to be an exercise in futility. As Gustavo Gutierrez suggests, "liberation in fact expresses the inescapable moment of radical change"[2] from the status-quo, while Foucault contends that the most people can hope for is more of the same. What, then, has Paris to do with Jerusalem?

Passing conclusive judgements on the labyrinth of Foucault's studies of modernity—or postmodernity—is not such a simple affair. His dystopia represent different but real moments in our present epoch and cannot be easily dismissed. Instead, we must wrestle with their degree of disclosure for our comprehension of society. A work such as *Discipline and Punish*, for example, describes the unheard-of penetration of instrumental rationality into the humanitarian discourses and institutions of the twentieth century. Power/knowledge, therefore, is not completely hostile to the analytical concerns of Marx, the Frankfurt School, or even Jürgen Habermas.[3] Although Foucault is less intent on salvaging a substantive or communicative forms of rationality, this factor does not necessarily exclude an emancipatory interest. Indeed, the sentiments of resistance that emerge from Foucault's genealogies are not merely epiphenomena, but articulate deliberations, firmly rooted in life experiences.

Foucault's implicit concern for emancipation establishes the basis for the comparison with liberation theology. It is perhaps surprising that the specific issues championed by Christian political theologians discover an ally in Foucault. Whereas the dialogue with critical theory illuminates an emancipatory interest, the exchange with liberation theology intimates a moral orientation that expands the religious significance of Foucault's work.

The Critical Encounter

It is a well-known fact that liberation theology's point of departure for its analysis of power is a critical response to American neo-colonialism and its developmental economic strategies for Latin America. The Latin experience of this political reality attests to the parasitic nature of Northern Capitalism: it succeeds at the expense of the oppressive suffering of the poor and marginalized nations.[4] The depth of this degradation is a "total social fact" (to borrow a phrase from Marcel Mauss), affecting Latin American culture, ethnicity, and religion. From within this situation, the world easily divides into oppressors and oppressed.[5] As Gutierrez expresses the matter,

> only a class analysis will enable us to see what is really involved in the opposition between oppressed countries and dominant peoples. To take into account only the confrontation between nations misrepresents and in the last analysis waters down the real situation. Thus the theory of dependence will take the wrong path and lead to deception if the analysis is not put within the framework of the worldwide class struggle.[6]

This basic Christian-Marxist reading of things points to the liberation of God's people through a "profound transformation"[7] of society, culture, and politics, one that may find expression as an indigenous socialism imbued with the moral vision of the Bible. In effect, liberation theology counters domination by advocating a revolutionary shift in relations of power.

The liberationist response to power, however, should not be interpreted as a straightforward translation of Marxist theory. As Gregory Baum suggests, liberationist concerns for the preferential option for the poor and the struggle toward the just society are motivated by a religious commitment to the Gospel message.[8] It is therefore founded upon a transcendent principle[9] that propels liberation theology beyond Marxist positivism and its one-sided materialism.[10] Nevertheless, liberationist thinkers affirm a sociology of conflict, oppression, and evil dedicated to the creation of a better society.[11]

From Foucault's perspective, the above analysis of power is based upon the dated and politically irrelevant notion of sovereignty. This "old" power is characterized as subject-centred, functioning within the parameters of command/obedience and domination/subjugation.[12] Here the task is to limit the actions and behaviour of both the sovereign and its subjects through laws, constitutions, and the threat of physical violence. For Foucault, the prohibitive conception of power fails to accurately represent the dynamics and ramifications of modern power practices. "If power were never anything but repressive, if it never did anything but say no," writes Foucault, "do you really think one would be brought to obey it?"[13] Thus Marxist variations of power analysis are theoretically inadequate, and "[w]e need to cut off the King's head"[14] of political theory, as it were.

In contrast to the sovereign position, Foucault juxtaposes "bio-power." This form of power alludes to surreptitious yet forceful societal practices that expand the efficient control *over* and *within* the human creature. It is a subject-less, self-perpetuating, and self-sufficient "micro-fascism"[15] that underscores the asymmetry "between the processes of power and the bodies that are crushed within them."[16] Foucault succinctly summarizes what these processes involve when he writes:

> Power must be analyzed as something which circulates, or rather as something which only functions in the form of a chain. It is never localized here or there, never in anybody's hands, never appropriated as a commodity or piece of wealth. Power is employed and exercised through a net-like organization. And, not only do individuals circulate between its threads; they are always in the position of simultaneously undergoing and exercising power. They are not only its inert or consenting target; they are always also the elements of its articulation.[17]

A fundamental element in this articulation is the normative knowledge of science and the humanities. These discourses support and are dependent upon amassing information for the production, classification, and organization of docile human types. In this way, knowledge, or "truth," is legitimated by successful power practices that, in turn, feed upon the status of a political "regime of truth."[18] The final result is the disciplinary society that generates techniques for monitoring and reforming human behaviour according to knowledges already oriented toward the perpetuation of those same practices.[19] Truth, therefore, is a fabrication of the Nietzschean "will to power."

A serious consequence of this notion of truth or power/knowledge is that we cannot challenge or limit our own political regime of truth by juxtaposing alternative, critical insights. The normative basis for liberation from coercive power complexes thus appears ineffectual.[20] Similarly, it seems that meaningful action, as liberating praxis, is also denied.[21] What, then, can be more antithetical to liberation theology than power/knowledge? According to Foucault, there can be no liberating truth of the Gospel, nor a revolutionary praxis of love that could be politically actualized. In light of these implications, Foucault's critical unmasking of instrumental rationality and its emancipatory tenor is effectively vanquished. Habermas has suggested that Foucault's work is seriously undermined by this performative contradiction, which illuminates an inherent irrationalism. The only way that Foucault's analytic of power can maintain any sense of credibility is to include a normative thrust, which of course Foucault denies.[22] Hence Foucault's agenda, at best, is "crypto-normative,"[23] thereby falling prey to the very categories of his own nebulous characterization of power/knowledge.

However, perhaps Habermas' criticisms are more telling of Foucault's ultimate concerns than destructive. That is, the *normative potential* evinced in Foucault's analysis may be retrieved and reconsidered in a way that is conscious of the circulation of power while remaining open to alternative, emancipatory configurations of power/knowledge. In many ways, this re-thinking of power constituted the course of Foucault's turn toward the subject in his later writings on sexuality.[24] This unfinished project can lead to some important speculations. However, I contend that the seeds of this revaluation already exist within his reflections on power and deserve to be fully explored.

The retrieval of the normative potential of Foucault's philosophy begins with an obvious point: a person who invests time and energy in writing, publishing, communicating to the public, and teaching in an articulate fashion is not irrational, but is attempting to impress the lives of others.[25] As Eugen Rosenstock-Heussy once noted, "any man who prints a book sends out an invitation: come and read and buy and learn and hear and digest and apply and understand."[26] The drive for understanding is something that Foucault experienced in relation to his own corpus of writings, as he was constantly reconsidering the aims and continuities of his diverse interests.

In this regard, Foucault did acknowledge that his power/knowledge configuration tended to be one-sided.[27] Yet, remaining on that side for a moment, there emerges an insight that admits a profound religious disposition. This involves the idea that knowledge is always tainted by some kind of power relation or structure, and that one's claims for carotid are curtailed by human finitude and the social construction of reality. From a Christian perspective, this circumspection of intellectual arrogance is bound with a profound sense of humility; with a deep appreciation of the ultimate mystery of life; and with a suspicion of the sin of self-sufficiency. Although these darker qualities have been "temptations of religion" as Charles Davis has explained, the "lust for certitude" is self-defeating. "Such self-enclosure violates the nature of religious faith," writes Davis, "which implies a self-transcending openness to total reality."[28] In this way, faith can include an ambiguity that is spiritually liberating.

A similar kind of self-enclosure, I feel, motivates Foucault's reserved acceptance of ideology-critique. As he remarks, "it always stands in virtual opposition to something else which is supposed to count as truth."[29] Moreover, it is a conception of truth unfettered by power, error, or illusion, which for Foucault is an epistemological fiction. However, the lie is put to this story when it is recognized that truth—as intellectual certitude—*necessarily excludes* not only other cognitive perspectives, but the very experiences upon which these alternative truths are based: the experiences of the poor, the marginalized, the deviant.[30]

This latter remark places us squarely within the concerns of liberation theology. Its own sense of religious humility, human finitude, and sin is related to the struggle for political emancipation in a way that echoes the thoughts of Foucault. The first point worth mentioning is that liberation theology affirms that sociological knowledge is *not* value neutral.[31] This judgement stems from the preferential option for the poor, which constitutes a novel epistemological approach and attempts to avoid the misleading ideal of establishing an epistemological privilege. In a self-involving manner, liberation theologians write through their experiences with the marginalized member of society. In turn, this "reveal[s] to them that the approach to one's own society is inevitably perspectival."[32] This position is confirmed by an attitude toward power reminiscent of Foucault as well. In this case, it is admitted that "the preferential option for the poor constitutes a critical principle that remains valid and operative after the revolution."[33] Thus, a circulating power is met on its own ground by abandoning the self-enclosed, anti-transcendent thrust of an intellectual certitude.

Nevertheless, for the Liberation Theologian there remains a possibility of overcoming power, while Foucault maintains that power is a constant dynamic of *any* social undertaking. This difference may be explained, in part, by the disparate social contexts that each position embodies. Foucault, writing out of a non-revolutionary situation, addresses his immanent critique to the entrenched bureaucratic monoliths of the Northern Hemisphere. In the South, the situation is radically different, and a shift in power relations would have a profound impact on current practices of domination. But aside from these qualifications, there is a more general challenge put by Foucault's power/knowledge that has yet to be fully appreciated by liberation and political theology. That is, the circulating nature of power demands that Christians attempt to move from faith toward public policy.[34] As Charles Davis expresses the matter,

> political theology manifests a tendency to leave faith as transcendent, soaring above the political sphere in eschatological flight, rather than making it enter more deeply than ever into political reality through a newly found self-reflective autonomy and responsibility of critical conscious Christians.[35]

If we take Davis' point seriously, along with Foucault's view of power, the question becomes *not how to eradicate power, but how to use it responsibly within the contingencies and exigencies of the political sphere*. This shifts our attention from political theory toward considerations of strategy. In the North American context, it may be that an indigenous socialism could prove inadequate to the task of transforming the bureaucratic, capitalist system, and that something more extreme is demanded. Political responsibility in the widest sense of the phrase—as caring for the overall direction and growth of society toward something different from the status-quo, something which may nurture human potential—may require an interim anarchy or rebellion, so as to combat the social evils at hand. This thought, at least, remains a distinct possibility, and it may be that Foucault's work can provide us with some norms and guidelines. It is to these guidelines that we now turn.

The Syntropic Encounter

The proceeding discussion seems to intimate that Foucault *did* hold that there is truth and knowledge deserving of our attention, but "that conceptions of what counts as true or false are complex and multileveled."[36] In other words, there may be different, more enabling configurations of power/knowledge that are dissociated from instrumental rationality and its practices. One such configuration is what we might call *resistance/subjugated knowledges*. Foucault explains the latter half of this complex in the following passage:

> Subjugated knowledges are…those blocs of historical knowledge which were present but disguised within the body of functionalist and systematizing theory and which criticism…has been able to reveal.
>
> On the other hand, I believe that by subjugated knowledges one should understand something else, something which in a sense is altogether different, namely, a whole set of knowledges that have been disqualified as inadequate to their task or insufficiently elaborated: naive knowledges, located low down on the hierarchy, beneath the required level of cognition of scientificity. I also believe that it is through the reemergence of those low-ranking knowledges…(such as that of the psychiatric patient, of the ill person,…that of the delinquent, etc.),…a differential knowledge incapable of unanimity and which owes its force only to the harshness with which it is opposed by everything surrounding it—that it is through the reappearance of this knowledge…that criticism performs its work.[37]

This quotation points out an elemental relationship between knowledge and life-experience. In this case, Foucault draws our attention to the lifeworld of the poor, the outcast, and the criminal. It is a knowing that arises from the victims of the disciplinarian society. These are historical, fragmented knowledges of local life struggles, which ally themselves with a genealogical scholarship for the purpose of creating a decisive, immanent critique of society. As such, subjugated knowledges do not represent a valuation of ignorance nor the undifferentiated consciousness, but stand for experientially based "antisciences" that counter the institutional centralization of scientific discourse with "the rude memory of their conflicts."[38]

At this juncture of our presentation, an obvious question suggests itself: is not this conception of subjugated knowledge similar to the preferential option for the poor? It seems clear to me that Foucault's excavations of modernity conform to many aspects of a sociology of evil. First, like liberation theology, Foucault's notion of subjugated knowledges is offered as a unique epistemological approach to the study of society. Second, it is firmly rooted in the struggles of communities and individuals. Third, these forgotten struggles resurface as "dangerous memories"[39] that show up the distortions and perversions of allowing these local knowledges to speak in their own voice and words.

On the other side of the coin, could we not also suggest that the preferential option for the poor represents an articulation of a subjugated knowledge? Consider again Gutierrez's critique of developmentalism. In one sense, he is protesting against the imposition of a standard that pretends to be concerned with the best interests of the Latin American people by transplanting North American capitalist modes of behaviour and thought. Furthermore, this "normal" state of affairs is defined by economists, scientists, and politicians tied to central institutions of power-control. In response to this situation, Gutierrez advocates the insurrection of a subjugated knowledge toward emancipation. "In order for...liberation to be authentic and complete, it has to be undertaken by the oppressed themselves and so must stem from their values proper to them."[40]

Gutierrez's statement, however, includes a reference to the possibility of a genuine praxis. Praxis, as a dialectic between experienced action and articulate response toward a meaningful involvement in history, concerns an empowerment of a subjugated knowledge as a "world building process."[41] As such, it is not merely a "differential knowledge incapable of unanimity,"[42] but a differential knowledge that forms community, inspires song and story, and compels solidarity. Thus, praxis "in a deeper sense, [is] to see the becoming of humankind as a process of human emancipation in history. It is to see humanity in search of a qualitatively different society in which it will be free of all servitude, in which it will be the artisan of its won destiny. It is to seek the building up of a *new humanity*."[43]

In light of this understanding of praxis and community, I believe we have come upon a lacuna between liberation theology and Foucault's philosophy that cannot be completely bridged. Still, there may be a partial closing of this gap in Foucault's notion of resistance. This term refers to various forms of rebellion against heterogeneous processes of normalization. It is an activity that exploits the interstices of modern power systems, interrupting their automation whenever the opportunity arises.[44] Liberation in this fashion really denotes a detachment from the status-quo through local struggles against injustice.[45] According to David Couzens Hoy, resistance as such can be supportive of qualitative change for society despite its anti-revolutionary stance.[46] In fact, Hoy contends that it is precisely this micro-level approach to social transformation that avoids fatalism. Totalized programmes for change will ultimately fail since the whole can never be altered through singular plans of action—modern society is too complex for such a tactic. "In fact we know from experience" writes Foucault, "that the claim to escape from the system of contemporary reality so as to produce the overall programmes of another society, of another thinking, another culture, another vision of the world, has led only to the return of the most dangerous traditions."[47] This perception of limited resistance is tied to Foucault's critique of universal rationality and metaphysics and the attempt to transcend the power/knowledge configuration. It is here, then, that we can underscore the relation between action and theory, which may result in a *fluid but oriented praxis*. It is fluid because "the theoretical and practical experience that we have of our limits and of the possibility of moving beyond them is always limited and determined; thus we are always in the position of beginning again."[48] Yet it is oriented because the subjugated knowledges present an experiential opportunity to challenge these limits via transgression. This praxis may be described then as "a patient labour giving form to our impatience for liberty."[49]

But what kind of form emerges from resistance/subjugated knowledge? Although Foucault often hesitates to predict the character of the transgressive society, he did intimate a very general vision. "It is possible that the rough outline of a future society is provided by the recent experiences with drugs, sex, communes, other forms of consciousness, and other forms if individuality. If scientific socialism emerged from the Utopias of the nineteenth century, it is possible that a real socialization will emerge, in the twentieth century, from *experiences*."[50] This statement in part qualifies Foucault's assertion that unanimity is impossible. Although complete concord and planned action may not be available nor desirable, it seems necessary that there at least be some sense of joint participation. As Foucault suggests, "we can't defeat the system through isolated actions; we must engage it on all fronts—the university, the prisons, and the domain of psychiatry—one after another since our forces are not strong enough for a simultaneous attack."[51] In short, it is a question of transgressive transformation of deconstructing the modern capitalist system, unit by unit, until nothing is left. It is a move toward a "new politics of truth"[52]—*subjugated truth*.

At first glance, what Foucault proposes is an anarchy devoid of an alternative replacement for the present political state. This position can hardly provide the foundation for a "world building process." But can we not enquire into its potential as a "jumping-off" point, as it were? From this angle, a number of practical and theological insights comes into view.

Practically, transgressive transformation is a deft response to modern capitalism and its bureaucratic structures. As Max Weber illustrates in *Economy and Society*, monocratic bureaucracy is the "root of the modern Western State."[53] It is designed to administer and control the mass society through an efficient technocratic rationality that is indispensable for the continued functioning of the status quo. As such, monocratic bureaucracy is interwoven with the growth of the capitalist system since they share the same aims and goals:

methods of production (i.e., specialization) and prosperity (i.e., voluminous output with the least possible effort and cost). In effect, it is a similar kind of ethos that Foucault describes in *Discipline and Punish*. But what is interesting here is Weber's reflection upon the potential for changing the modern state. He writes:

> Only by revision in every field—political, religious, economic, etc.—to small scale organizations would it be possible to any considerable extent to escape [the bureaucratic] influence.[54]

This suggestion, of course, brings to mind the sociological reflections of Peter Berger. He advocated the religious retreat from political activism toward the cultivation of the private, interior needs of the faithful, so as to cope with the dehumanizing trends of the bureaucratic state.[55] The privatization of meaning, however, is not what Foucault has proposed. The significant point to be stressed is that Foucault—like Weber—comprehends that a profound or ultimate transformation of modern society will not occur by replacing one bureaucracy or institution by another of a similar form. The capitalist society cannot be countered by its mirror opposite, i.e., socialism, but by its complete opposite: *power practices that undermine the totalizing paradigm and its institutions*.

Foucault's transgressive transformation is likewise not without its theological resonance. The first theological story that suggests itself here is the death and resurrection of Jesus. That is, the old society and power must die in order for the new to arise. Another story concerns the political orientation and activities of Jesus. In many ways, did not Jesus illuminate transcendence through transgressive transformation of the status quo? Did he not wander in small groups, engaging in sporadic and local struggles with the political and community leaders of Judah? There was no attempt to organize an institution to replace the existing structures; instead, Jesus not only preached *metanoia* but lived it, allowing those around him to experience liberation through a radical reorientation of perception and life practices.

These negative experiences of the divine do admit a certain degree of complementarity with the anarchistic position. But with the richness of the Christian tradition and life, this represents but one moment. To hold this moment to be the quintessence of faith creates a distortative closure contrary to the openness of faith. And it is exactly this openness that distinguishes faith from the unfaith of nihilism.[56] Yet is this not the thrust of Foucault's resistance/subjugated knowledges? Although it would be ridiculous to assert that Foucault was a closet Christian, his *difficult discourse on emancipation* is not completely devoid of hope: "thus we are always in the position of beginning again."[57] How, then, might the liberation and political theologian situate Foucault's work so as to enter a concrete and constructive dialogue with him? Or how might the religious thinker begin again?

The Affirmative Encounter

The answer to the above query has been lurking in the background throughout the essay, and now deserves to be directly confronted: that is, *Foucault as a parabolic thinker*. My point of departure for this discussion is John Dominic Crosson's influential work, *The Dark Interval*. In this study, Crossan attempts to demonstrate that the *subversive* parables of Jesus evoke a reader—or hearer—response hermeneutics[58] that brings to bear a negative connection between the Kingdom of God—as a spiritual force of divine presence—and our day-to-day world. As Crossan remarks,

> I would suggest that the connection is summed up in the maxim: Parables give God room. The parables of Jesus are *not* historical allegories telling us God acts with mankind; neither are they moral example-stories telling us how to act before God and towards one another. They are stories which shatter the deep structure of our accepted world and thereby render clear and evident to us the relativity of story itself. They remove our defences and make us vulnerable to God. It is only in such experiences that God can touch us, and only in such moments does the kingdom of God arrive. My own term for this relationship is transcendence.[59]

This interpretation of the parables discovers an experiential basis in liberation theology. The theologians' *abrupt awakening* to the plight of the poor, their analysis of the socio-political (deep) structures that support this situation, and a shameful awareness of their own participation in such a state of affairs constituted a world-shattering experience, compelling a fundamental reorientation in Christian praxis and theology. These theologians and Christians returned to the Biblical accounts of God's action in history, and to the concerns of the praxis of Jesus, to retrieve a subjugated knowledge: the preferential option for the poor. In short, the parabolic experience transforms the present through the intervention of an unknown, free, and open future that ushers in a divine moment. As a present experience oriented toward that which is yet to come, it intimates a correspondence of incarnation and eschatology. As Gregory Baum has suggested, "God's presence is explosive, unsettling, empowering, future creating: it transcends all the prisons that humans have built for themselves and triumphs over all domination and injustice."[60]

It is perhaps fortuitous that Baum should mention the transcendence of human prisons, for such is the underlying concern of Foucault's *Discipline and Punish*: the transcendence of "humane" prisons. In this study, Foucault demonstrates that modern society is not morally progressive, despite its humanitarian discourses and their impact upon the reform of institutions such as the prison, the hospital, or the school. Indeed, the idea of domination through normalization shatters the deep structures of the humanistic and liberal world. Foucault's analysis of power/knowledge undermines the certitude of ideology-critique and of Marxist totalization. It is for this reason that I contend that Foucault is a contemporary instance of a parabolic thinker.

However, can it be said that Foucault's parables "make room for God?"

Conclusion

To a certain extent, this essay has tried to demonstrate that this is indeed the case, by illuminating the points of contact with liberation theology and by intimating how Foucault's resistance/subjugated knowledges express an emancipatory interest that counters the bureaucratic and capitalist systems of the Northern Hemisphere. In this sense, we can suggest that *transgressive transformation* is a variation of *parabolic transformation*, and therefore, includes a transcendent moment that opens the present to divine encounter.

It is certainly credible to wonder how profound this correspondence really is. After all, liberation and political theologians recognize that we cannot live by subversive parable alone. The open future that rushes in through the parabolic experience also includes a divine imperative to be fulfilled by a way of life, grounded in the word of God. That is, fragmentation is ultimately overcome by a spiritual trust in the divine presence that leads toward wholeness, community, and love. In fact without this drive toward reconstitution, the parabolic experience is without effect. The impact of the parable depends upon the hearer's tight involvement in the common discourse of a community. As such the parable represents an *immanent critique* that encourages reorientation, but it is a reorientation that avails itself of alternative sources of meaning, slumbering with the traditions of the community. Hence the *retrieval* of the preferential option for the poor from the Christian tradition by liberation theology. This retrieval, however, is not the resurrection of some pristine doctrine or experience, but a new creation in history. *It is the expansion of the horizon of meaning through a transcendent experience made possible by the disruptive awakening of God's presence with the poor.*

This reorientation of theology, though, also leads to various dialogues with other kinds of thought and tradition, such as the Marxist tradition and the Frankfurt School, both of which include their own parabolic resonance. I have tried to argue here that Foucault's work should be considered in a similar vein, but with a stronger emphasis on the religious significance of his thought. As such, the question is *not only* "how can Foucault's insights help the Christian political theologian better express his or her critique of modern forms of domination?" but also "why should Foucault's parabolic studies of modernity lead to a reconsideration of Christian theology and praxis?" The answer I have suggested is that Foucault's power/knowledge or resistance/subjugated knowledges expands the horizon of meaning for political theology while maintaining a point of identity with its moral urgency and its desire to create a new society. *In other words, Foucault's work points toward the disruptive presence of God.*

Notes

1. Charles Taylor, "Foucault on Freedom and Truth," in *Foucault: A Critical Reader*, ed. David Couzens Hoy (Oxford: Basil Blackwell, 1986), 70.
2. Gustavo Gutierrez, *A Theology of Liberation: History, Politics, and Salvation*, trans. Sister Caridad Inda and John Eagleson (Maryknoll, NY: Orbis Books, 1988), 17.
3. See Mark Poster, *Critical Theory and Poststructuralism: In Search of A Context* (Ithaca, NY: Cornell University Press), 25–26.
4. Gutierrez, *A Theology of Liberation*, 51.
5. Dennis P. McCann, *Christian Realism and Liberation Theology: Practical Theologies in Creative Conflict* (Maryknoll, NY: Orbis Books, 1981), 145.
6. Gutierrez, *A Theology of Liberation*, 54.
7. Ibid., 54.
8. Gregory Baum, *Theology and Society* (New York: Paulist Press, 1987), 119.
9. Ibid., 120.
10. Ibid., 127.
11. Ibid., 157–178.
12. Michel Foucault, *Power/Knowledge: Selected Interviews and Other Writings*, trans. Colin Gordon and others (New York: Pantheon Books, 1980), 96.
13. Ibid., 119.

14. Ibid., 121.
15. Michael Walzer, "The Politics of Michel Foucault," in *Foucault: A Critical Reader*, ed. David Couzens Hoy (Oxford: Basil Blackwell, 1986), 63.
16. Jürgen Habermas, *The Philosophical Discourse of Modernity: Twelve Lectures*, trans. Frederick G. Lawrence (Cambridge, Mass.: MIT Press, 1987), 285.
17. Foucault, *Power/Knowledge*, 98.
18. Ibid., 131.
19. Michel Foucault, *Discipline and Punish: The Birth of the Prison*, trans. Alan Sheridan (New York: Vintage Books, 1979).
20. Taylor, "Foucault on Freedom and Truth," 94.
21. Sheldon S. Wolin, "On the Theory and Practice of Power," in *After Foucault: Humanistic Knowledge, Postmodern Challenges*, ed. Jonathan Arac (New Brunswick: Rutgers University Press, 1988), 200.
22. Habermas, *The Philosophical Discourse of Modernity*, 273–279.
23. Ibid., 276.
24. See, for example, Arnold J. Davidson, "Archaeology, Genealogy, Ethics," in *Foucault: A Critical Reader*, ed. David Couzens Hoy (Oxford: Basil Blackwell, 1986), 221–233.
25. According to Mark Poster, one such person is Jürgen Habermas himself. As Poster remarks in *Critical Theory and Poststructuralism*, "Habermas appropriates the poststructuralist critique of reason for his own ends" (20), as evinced in Habermas' text *The Philosophical Discourse of Modernity*. For a more complete analysis of this appropriation, see Poster, *Critical Theory and Poststructuralism*, 12–33.
26. Eugen Rosenstock-Heussy, *Speech and Reality* (Norwich, Vt: Argo Books, 1970), 61.
27. This is noted in Habermas, *The Philosophical Discourse of Modernity*, 273.
28. Charles Davis, *Temptations of Religion* (New York: Harper and Row, 1973), 15.
29. Foucault, *Power/Knowledge*, 118.
30. Davis, *Temptations of Religion*, 10, 17.
31. Baum, *Theology and Society*, 117.
32. Ibid., 118.
33. Ibid., 120.
34. One exception to this rule is Gregory Baum, *Compassion and Solidarity: The Church for Others* (Montréal: CBC Enterprises, 1987), 64–69.
35. Charles Davis, *Theology and Political Society* (Cambridge: Cambridge University Press, 1980), 74.
36. David Couzens Hoy, "Foucault: Modern or Postmodern?" in *After Foucault: Humanistic Knowledge, Postmodern Challenges*, ed. Jonathan Arac (New Brunswick: Rutgers University Press, 1988), 14.
37. Foucault, *Power/Knowledge*, 83.
38. Ibid., 83.
39. See J.B. Metz, *Faith in History and Society: Toward a Practical Fundamental Theology*, trans. David Smith (New York: Crossroad, 1980), 88.
40. Gutierrez, *A Theology of Liberation*, 57.
41. Baum, *Theology and Society*, 123.

42. Foucault, *Power/Knowledge*, 82.
43. Gutierrez, *A Theology of Liberation*, 56.
44. Wolin, "On the Theory and Practice of Power," 181.
45. Ian Hacking, "The Archaeology of Foucault," in *Foucault: A Critical Reader*, ed. David Couzens Hoy (Oxford: Basil Blackwell, 1986), 39.
46. Hoy, "Foucault: Modern or Postmodern?", 35–36.
47. Michel Foucault, "What is Enlightenment?" trans. Robert Hurley and others, in *Ethics: Subjectivity and Truth*, vol. 1 of *The Essential Works of Michel Foucault, 1954–1984*, ed. Paul Rabinow (New York: The New Press, 1997), 316.
48. Ibid., 316–317.
49. Ibid., 319.
50. Michel Foucault, *Language, Counter-Memory, Practice: Selected Essays and Interviews*, trans. Donald F. Bouchard and Sherry Simon (Ithaca, NY: Cornell University Press, 1977), 231.
51. Ibid., 230.
52. Foucault, *Power/Knowledge*, 133.
53. Max Weber, *Economy and Society*, vol. 1 (New York: Bedminster Press, 1968), 223.
54. Ibid., 224.
55. See Peter L. Berger, *The Sacred Canopy* (Garden City, NY: Doubleday Anchor Books, 1967), 129–153.
56. Charles Davis, "Our Modern Identity: The Formation of the Self," *Modern Theology* 6 (1990): 168.
57. Foucault, "What is Enlightenment?" 317.
58. Roger Lundin, Anthony C. Thiselton, and Clarence Walhout, *The Responsibility of Hermeneutics* (Grand Rapids, MI: Wm. B. Eerdmans Publishing Company, 1985), 79–113.
59. John Dominic Crossan, *The Dark Interval: Towards a Theology of Story* (Allen, TX: Argus, 1975), 121–122.
60. Baum, *Theology and Society*, 140.

Essay Three

On The Moral-Existential Facet of Religious Studies Today

IN THE most general sense, the social scientific study of religion explores religious phenomena in terms external to the traditions, ideas, beliefs, symbols, and practices under study. Here the notion of "religion" is grasped as a finite human construct that lends itself to rational re-articulation along social, cultural, political, philosophical, historical, psychological, or naturalistic lines of enquiry. The end point of this manifold approach is to develop *theories* of religion which can clarify complicated human behaviours in accord with the directives of academic scholarship. Such "Theories remain multiple," to cite Craig Calhoun, "not because we are confused or have not yet reached correct scientific understanding of the problems before us, but because all problems...can be seen in different ways."[1] Otherwise put, it is unlikely that a single theory could totally account for the intricacies of religious life and thought or exhaust all the vital issues that call for sustained attention.

In keeping with this valuation of diverse theory, I hold that *part* of the purpose of religious studies is to facilitate the reflexive exploration of moral-existential frameworks of religious meaning in view of contemporary socio-cultural tensions, problems, and contradictions. The task here, it should be stressed, is not to provide definitive answers to complex questions. Rather, the aim is to enable an open discussion about the truth, value, and purpose of human(e) being by delving into some of the more penetrating religious responses to the indefiniteness of the lived life. Toward that end, I propose a critical examination of first order religious discourses (i.e., primary expressions of particular faiths, scriptural writings, fundamental ritual practices, etc.), second order religious discourses (i.e., theologies, religious philosophies, devotional tracts, manuals, etc.), and third order religious discourses (i.e., inspired philosophies, psychologies, arts and literature, etc.) in relation to an analysis of the present that will generate a *fourth order discourse* constructively connected to, though not merely a conduit for, religious sources of meaning. In this fashion, religious studies may contribute to what Calhoun identifies as the essential challenge for the social sciences today: that effort to surpass the re-presentation of familiar social facts toward a critical though creative re-visioning of how these "facts" could be different or improved.[2] What I am calling the "moral-existential facet of religious studies," then, has the potential to amplify the critical import of this discipline as a whole.

Yet with this summary of things a persisting methodological dilemma comes to mind: can religious studies agree to a moral-existential facet that highlights the religious "truth, value, and purpose of human(e) being" without raising the spectre of an undisclosed theological agenda? Does such an approach not require an appropriate relation to theological traditions, methods, and goals? If we answer yes here, might the dilemma be resolved by creating some disciplinary space for the study of theology within religious studies? Yet if we take this tack, what features serve to warrant the separation of religious studies from theological programmes? Or does the answer to this impasse demand that the social scientific study of religion abstain from all questions of meaning as Donald Wiebe insists?[3] These queries and suspicions cannot be easily dismissed. When Charles Davis first considered the issue in his controversial essay "The Reconvergence of Theology and Religious Studies,"[4] for instance, he concluded by totally subordinating the academic study of religion to a theoretical theology deemed integral to the objective analysis of religion. It is so, Davis asserted, because that which substantiates the religious object as real and true—namely, God, or Ultimate Reality—demands a method germane to the data under study. For without such a method to deal with the unique qualities that distinguish religious phenomena from the stuff of everyday life, religious studies loses its academic point, purpose, and goal. For this reason Davis argued that "The science of religion…has to be completed by a philosophico-theological discourse."[5] A major problem with this proposal, however, is that it logically requires a faith-commitment from the student of religion. As Davis put it, "those without a taste for the divine"[6] can hardly be expected to be "sensitive interpreter[s] of religious data."[7] Now this claim is highly problematic because; first, it deflects critical questions about the purpose of religious faith by mandating an inaccessible privilege—a personal experience of God—as the key to understanding, elucidating, and communicating the "real" meaning of religion; second, because it doesn't duly consider the potential for religious studies to examine issues of religious truth, value, and purpose though perhaps quite differently than theology. Against Davis, then, it is the purpose of this essay to draft the form of this difference as the "moral-existential facet of religious studies."

The first section of this study takes up the moral-existential facet of religious studies in relation to the modern fear of meaninglessness as a socio-cultural motivation for analysing sources of religious insight. To do so thoughtfully yet non-theologically, however, requires a new mode of critical deliberation that can stimulate creative speculation. Toward that end, the second section proceeds with a review of Michel Foucault's essay, "What is Enlightenment?" My concern here is to accent Foucault's notion of transgressive transformation as the critical approach most germane to the moral-existential facet of religious studies. By way of demonstrating the value of this Foucauldian design, section three sets out to untangle the postmodern contingencies motivating Jürgen Habermas' peculiar assessment of religious life and thought. Here we learn that the religious, for Habermas, serves to keep postmodern philosophy in check—an idea which also works to betray Habermas' want of a religious social ethic for the promotion of a more compassionate society. This revelation then clears the way for a concluding reflection on Emmanuel Levinas' unique view of the religio-ethical as the transgressive transformation of Habermas' attitude and stance. On the hither side of this particular innovation, however, resides further work for the moral-existential facet of religious studies today.

Religious Studies and the Modern Fear of Meaninglessness

If it's at all true, as Thomas Helm reports, that students drawn to his introductory course on Christianity want to learn how this tradition has "shaped and continues to shape human existence,"[8] then the study of religion should entail in part, and only in part, an open deliberation about the truth, value, and purpose of human(e) being by investigating the more perceptive religious responses to the ambiguities of existence. This reflexive exploration of what I am calling "moral-existential frameworks of religious meaning," does not aim to ground religious studies as a whole nor to govern the quest for meaning in its entirety. Humanity's "will to meaning," to borrow Viktor Frankl's expression,[9] is *not* always already religious. Nevertheless, the moral-existential moment of religious studies is far from arbitrary. One important incentive for the academic study of religion is linked to a diminished sense of life-orientation resulting from the marginalization of religion in the modern age. As Robert Spivey observes, religious studies prospers in accord with the deflation of formally recognized religious institutions: "When the church and synagogue are weak," he remarks, then the academic study of religion "will be strong because people will be questioning…their traditional religious roots."[10] Yet beyond this engagement of lapsed forms of life that continue to possess intellectual and emotional purchase, there resides a more involved disturbance which better situates Spivey's point: namely, the modern fear of meaninglessness. So framed, the academic study of religion can be arranged to include discerning meditations on prevailing forms of *Angst* in concert with religious sources capable of dealing with such anxiety in terms of its cause, import, consequences, and possible dissolution.

To be sure, this overburdened approach to the contemporary significance of religion hardly seems to inspire.[11] Still the point remains that the threat of meaninglessness has been and continues to be a constitutive feature of modernity in marked contrast to other epochs and cultures. According to Charles Taylor, the modern existential predicament could not have been thoroughly grasped by persons living in earlier periods of history.[12] The worry of succumbing to an overwhelming sense of emptiness, for example, would have run up against a moral-religious worldview impervious to such a metaphysical assault. Taylor therefore concludes that the problem of life-meaning is plainly a component of our unfolding cultural agenda.[13] It is in light of this impression that religious studies may ascertain part of its *raison d'être* today.

Of course opposition to this proposal is not far off. In their conclusion to *Religious Studies in Ontario*, authors Remus, James, and Fraikin elicit Ivan Strenki's warning that religious studies departments must be wary of becoming "the walk-in therapy centre for the university," to the potential neglect of "knowledge and education, hard thinking and good writing..."[14] In other words, it is not the responsibility of religious studies to remedy personal psychological problems. Granted the prudential bearing of this advice, its cautionary thrust need not derail the recognition of related though unremitting issues that can situate the moral-existential facet of religious studies as a rigorous inspection of shared adversities affecting society at large, cultural expression, the academy, theory construction, and so on.

Take, for example, the idea of a "dialectic of Enlightenment." As Max Horkheimer and Theodor Adorno decipher it, the "promise" of Enlightenment—that is, the freedom and autonomy of the human being over and against a fully transparent world—yields an oppressive, often violent approach to existence. It does so because the very notion of "enlightenment" implies that no thing, nothing considered real, is allowed to endure as uncertain, mysterious, or "Other" in the face of the rational, controlling Subject. However, given the ineradicable realities of natural disaster, historical contingency, and human unpredictability, a power struggle develops fostering the dominance of an instrumental reason that equates meaning with the skill to regulate calamity, anomaly, and heterogeneity. Yet it is precisely with this equation, Horkheimer and Adorno assert, that the modern Enlightenment unwittingly duplicates the primitive urge to reduce everything other than itself to an identifiable sameness that can be immanently mastered. Thus, despite all claims to intellectual, moral, and technical progress beyond the lowly religio-mythical worldview, the Enlightenment ultimately decrees that

> there is nothing new under the sun, because all the pieces in the meaningless game have been played, and all the great thoughts have already been thought, and because all possible discoveries can be construed in advance and all men are decided on adaptation as the means to self-preservation—that dry sagacity merely reproduces that fantastic wisdom which it supposedly rejects: the sanction of a fate that in retribution relentlessly remakes what has already been.[15]

There is no denying that *Dialectic of Enlightenment* represents one of the Frankfurt School'' "blackest of books," as Habermas describes it,[16] nor is it the only rejoinder to the Enlightenment worthy of thorough examination. Nonetheless, the *conjoncture* of pernicious historical-material forces and ideas that the authors indict as nihilistic cannot be intelligently overlooked. So even Habermas—whose theory of communicative action is constructed in direct opposition to *Dialectic of Enlightenment*—concedes the gravity of Horkheimer and Adorno's thesis. For given the dysfunctional consequences of technology and a systems-based mass society in our day-to-day lives, Habermas has no problem seeing why the "theories gaining in influence today are primarily those that try to show how the very forces…from which modernity once derived its self-consciousness and its utopian expectations, are in actuality turning autonomy into dependence, emancipation into oppression, and reason into irrationality."[17] In effect, the dialectic of Enlightenment denotes a disturbing socio-cultural configuration that impedes critical thought and expression as well as human happiness. And it is in precise view of these kinds of deep-seated crises that the moral-existential facet of religious studies acquires its basic focus and direction. For in a situation where "destructive forces" twist "autonomy into dependence, emancipation into oppression, and reason into irrationality," the moral-existential facet of religious studies gains emphasis as a free forum in which to discuss and debate such dilemmas. Thus on this side of a cultural exhaustion that presages philosophical despair, religious studies nurtures the diffusion of latent insight to the benefit of social criticism.

Religious Studies as Transgressive Transformation

How, then, to develop a non-theological method specific to the moral-existential facet of religious studies? What is required here is a flexible model of critical deliberation that can think with and through socio-cultural change and its justificatory discourses while also searching out different analytical configurations whose dissimilarity exhibits the prospect of notable change. The cultivation of this prospect may reside in and between those multiple, overlapping social worlds that distinguish modern pluralism. With due historical designation and critical-philosophic awareness, these worlds could be creatively juxtaposed to dislodge the habitual and expand the possible.[18] Such an investigation would thus help the knowing and acting subject to take serious stock of the present while resisting its identification as the final expression of all there is or could be.[19]

One important model for this type of deliberation is advanced in Michel Foucault's essay, "What is Enlightenment?"[20] Taking his inspiration from Kant, Foucault circumscribes a notion of philosophical interrogation that discerns the import of the present moment as a "difference in history and as motive for a particular philosophical task..."[21] What is the contemporary "difference" and "motive" for Foucault? How does he envision its "particular philosophical task"? Otherwise stated, "What is Enlightenment *Now*?"

As Foucault reads the situation, there does exist a vital form of philosophical thought that is historically rooted in the Enlightenment. However, its present manifestation, he says, has nothing to do with the dogmatic urge to reduce the Enlightenment to a specific doctrine, theory, or even an accumulated body of knowledge.[22] No, Enlightenment now is motivated by a "permanent reactivation of an attitude—that is, of a philosophical ethos that could be described as a permanent critique of our historical era."[23] By appealing to this ethos Foucault not only radicalizes the Kantian moment within contemporary thought, but does so by recasting its negative design into a positive construct that is no less critical. For if the Kantian task is to grasp the rational limits of knowledge as universal, necessary, and obligatory ones, then the Foucauldian version seizes upon the singular, contingent, and arbitrary factors at work *within* what is proclaimed to be universal, necessary, and obligatory. In other words, all discourses are inextricably constrained by particular conditions of occurrence which are seldom factored into the identity and shape of these discourses. Indeed, these kinds of conditions are usually suppressed. With their critical-philosophic discovery and historical analysis, however, the discourses in question are shorn of all claims to "Truth Eternal," exposed as immanently finite, and made vulnerable to problematization, experimentation, change, and transformation. Thus, "The point...is to transform the critique conducted in the form of necessary limitation into a practical critique that takes the form of a possible crossing-over [*franchissement*]."[24]

In effect, the present Enlightenment can be stylized as a form of transgressive transformation that does not reject the "limit attitude"[25] of critical philosophy as such, but explores the ways in which this attitude is subject to restrictions in itself.[26] Far from determining inescapable constraints or, following from this recognition, proving to be epistemologically distressing, these restrictions mark the historically engendered peripheries that invite the expansion of different ideals beyond the established limit, raising the hope for new beginnings. Says Foucault:

> criticism is no longer going to be practised in the search for formal structures with universal value, but rather as a historical investigation into the events that have led us to constitute ourselves and to recognize ourselves as subjects of what we are doing, thinking, saying. In that sense, this criticism...will not seek to identify the universal structures of all knowledge or of all possible moral action, but will seek to treat the instances of discourse that articulate what we think, say, and do as so many historical events. And this critique...will not deduce from the form of what we are what it is possible for us to do and to know; but it will separate out, from the contingency that has made us what we are, *the possibility of no longer being, doing, or thinking what we are, do, or think.*[27]

While there is a great deal more that one must examine in order to fully explain Foucault's position, enough has been said to entertain its significance for the moral-existential facet of religious studies. To start with, Foucault's emphasis on the inconspicuous, historically bounded interests that shape human discourse encourages a reassessment of the role of religious meaning within modernity. For if this role is fairly profiled as a dissimilarity that signals the chance for workable change, gone is the quick assumption that shifts in socio-cultural formation constitute certain steps in the march of an irreversible secularism. Gone, too, is the forced conjecture that such variations always lend themselves to re-symbolization as yet another phase of the supernatural expressed in time. What is not discarded, however, is the assortment of ways that human beings fashion and realize themselves as historical "subjects of what [they] are doing, thinking, saying." Insofar that this fashioning and realization has historically involved a strong religious component, its examination is vital for understanding identity formation.[28] And insofar that the crisis of the modern identity has involved a trivialization or rejection of this religious component, then it is historically transfigured into an effective antipode that facilitates the process of "no longer being, doing, or thinking what we are, do, or think." That is, religious meaning serves to extend different ideals that entreat the critical aptitude for new beginnings.[29] This fresh perception of things does not necessarily imply the construction of a new religious identity. Rather, it intends the opportunity for a different self-understanding instigated by religious sources of meaning brought to bear on a particular problematic.

To be sure, this approach installs a form of historical perspectivism that appears to undermine the normative basis for critique by rejecting the idea of purely rational, context-transcending claims to universal validity. But as Levinas reminds us, "There is an excellence in time that would be lost in eternity."[30] Part of that excellence which Foucault confers is a valuation of a practically oriented notion of "experimentation." By experimentation or the "experimental attitude," Foucault remarks, "I mean that this work done at the limits of ourselves must, on the one hand, open up a realm of historical enquiry and, on the other, put itself to the test of…contemporary reality, both to grasp the points where change is possible and desirable, and to determine the precise form this change should take."[31] What this criterion implores is a regard for speculative breakthrough and intellectual growth that exceeds positions found problematic by articulating others that seem to be less so. In a tentative sense, historical perspectivism "does not loose the stamp of truth," to quote the young Horkheimer,[32] but can be pictured as inventing "truing"[33] patterns of practical thought which, over time, can be gauged as temporarily settled achievements of "Enlightenment Now."

The Postmodern Contingencies of Habermas' Critique of Religion

In order to clarify the direction, focus, and method of the moral-existential facet of religious studies, I now undertake its demonstration by interrogating Jürgen Habermas' peculiar comments on religious life and thought, initiating its "transgressive transformation" via Emmanuel Levinas' interpretation of ethics in the next section of the essay. As an experimental exercise straining to enunciate the "points where change is possible and desirable, and to determine the precise form this change should take," this interrogation juxtaposes disparate patterns of life-orientation that help to "separate out, from the contingency that has made us what we are, *the possibility of no longer being, doing, or thinking what we are, do, or think."* Herein lies the talent of religious studies as a theoretical labour exceeding the re-presentation of familiar social facts in order to effect a critical though creative re-visioning of how these "facts" could be different or improved.

As early as 1971, Habermas insisted that "Postmetaphysical thought," that is, intersubjective forms of rational argumentation regulated by speech-immanent claims to universal validity, "does not dispute determinate theological affirmations; instead it asserts their meaninglessness."[34] In marked contrast to this stance, Habermas' most recent response is strikingly tolerant. As he puts it, for anyone schooled in the tradition of German Idealism "there is excluded from the start an approach that would merely objectify Jewish and Christian traditions..." [35] Yet despite this candid point of departure, Habermas finally decides that theology cannot accommodate itself to postmetaphysical thought lest it abandon the very thing which substantiates its claim to be the *logos* of the *theos*: namely, the experience and language of an extraordinary divine reality. Along side this conclusion, however, Habermas prescribes a rather curious role for the religious in the postmetaphysical age. Observes Habermas:

> ...ordinary life, now fully profane, by no means becomes immune to the shattering and subversive intrusion of extraordinary events. Viewed from without, religion, which has largely been deprived of its worldview functions, is still indispensable in ordinary life for *normalizing intercourse with the extraordinary*. For this reason,...[p]hilosophy, even in its postmetaphysical form, will be able neither to replace nor repress religion as long as religious language is the bearer of a semantic content that is inspiring and even indispensable, for this content...continues to resist translation into reasoning discourses.[36]

In this passage, Habermas is trying to secure a couple of interrelated points within a single thematic that unfolds in an extremely complex way. The thematic concerns the inherent unpredictability of human life—a difficult issue that has continually shadowed Habermas' penchant for systematic reason. In response to this pressure, Habermas here arranges the religious as an ordered moment within his system for the a-rational *as* a-rational. Thus religion, for Habermas, "indispensably" recapitulates the extraordinary dimensions of human existence within its "inspiring" semantic content. Of course this content cannot be appended to "the philosophical discourse of modernity." However, it can serve quite well as that which "normalizes" the modern intercourse with the extraordinary. But what, exactly, does this charge amount to? Why does

Habermas contend that such normalization is even required? What postmetaphysical purpose does it serve? What are the inconspicuous historically bounded interests that shape this peculiar directive?

The fact that the ordinary human life is not exempt from the stress and strain of "extraordinary events," remains for Habermas a constant—not only as fact, but as a source of philosophical confusion. "Since early Romanticism," he notes, "limit experiences of an aesthetic and mystical kind have always been claimed for the purpose of a rapturous transcendence of the subject."[37] This secular reclamation of religious experience is explained by Habermas as one kind of response to the reflexive and socio-cultural fragmentation precipitated by modernity. While the subjective freedom and ethical autonomy heralded by the modern age procures emancipation from past pressures and traditional restrictions, it also triggers an "alienation from the totality of an ethical context of life."[38] It is against this unfortunate effect that an aesthetic model of thought is advanced as an ersatz spirituality,[39] one that receives its consummate form from Nietzsche. "What Nietzsche calls the 'aesthetic phenomenon'," writes Habermas, "is disclosed in…a decentered subjectivity set free from everyday conventions of perceiving and acting. Only when the subject *loses* itself,…when it is stirred by the shock of the sudden,…when the…norms of daily life have broken down,…only then does the world of the unforseen and the absolutely astonishing open up…"[40] With this stylization of the extraordinary as philosophy, intersubjective forms of rational argumentation regulated by speech-immanent claims to universal validity are effectively eclipsed. Yet despite this obfuscation, admits Habermas, the allure of a teaching "with religiously and aesthetically toned ecstasy, finds an audience in circles of intellectuals who are prepared to make their *sacrificium intellectus* on the alter of their needs for orientation."[41]

The "circle of intellectuals" that Habermas targets are the postmodern philosophers who have allowed the extraordinary to rear its ugly head once again under the banner of "deconstruction." Considering the work of Jacques Derrida, Habermas submits that "The rebellious labour of deconstruction" means to "overthrow the primacy of logic over rhetoric."[42] With this inversion, two basic factors come into play that evince Derrida's "*sacrificium intellectus*." First, the priority of rhetoric frees Derrida to evaluate the essence of human communication as a poetic exercise "in world disclosure."[43] Second, the focus on disclosure blurs differences that delimit genre-types and academic disciplines. Thus science, philosophy, and literary criticism dissolve into an amorphous *Urschrift*[44] that disables rational critique. This deferral of accountable argument via playful rhetoric, concludes Habermas, betrays a "desire to *overdraw* th[e] aesthetic experience, to totalize the contact with the extraordinary, to absorb the everyday. Everything that piles up as problems in the world…is supposed to be reduced to a mere function of the opening of ever newer horizons of experience and of different ways of seeing things."[45]

According to Habermas then, Derrida, like Nietzsche, loses sight of those intersubjective forms of rational argumentation regulated by speech-immanent claims to universal validity. Yet in contrast to his judgement of Nietzsche, Habermas submits that Derrida does not promote a "New Paganism"[46] because of the Judaic mystical tradition that shapes deconstruction. The import of an *Urschrift*, for instance, is said to evoke "the metaphor of…the book of the world, which points to the hard-to-read, painstakingly to be deciphered handwriting of God."[47] What this deciphering announces is a notion of religious tradition as the ever changing, though ultimately delayed event of Revelation.[48] For Habermas, this restoration of "Being" to its monotheistic site[49] partially saves Derrida from that purely "aesthetic ecstasy [that] finds expression in the stunning and dizzying effects of (the illuminating) shock."[50]

Undoubtedly, the above exposition says more about Habermas than it does about Derrida.[51] That, however, is more than enough for us. For what this examination reveals is Habermas' phobia of postmodern thought as a heedless and frantic metaphysico-mystical vision of things that regrettably passes as rigorous critique. It is this concern that drives Habermas' opposition to Derrida's one-sided affirmation of rhetoric. For with this endorsement, problem solving language is displaced by a quixotic poetic of play. To mistake this play as the standard bearer of criticism, however, is to couple reason to the extraordinary, enticing a promiscuous confusion of distinct value spheres.[52] Habermas' designation of the religious as the normalizing factor of extraordinary events, language, and thought, then, is intended to avert conceptual bedlam by keeping the likes of Nietzsche and Derrida in their proper place, namely, the cult of the religious. Thus, the Romantic child of religion become postmodern is disciplined by returning it to the genitor: herein lies its redemption.

Of course it is highly debatable whether postmodern thought in general, or deconstruction in particular, can be dismissed as a pseudo-religious phenomena that closes ranks with the counter-Enlightenment. Against Habermas, both Christopher Norris and Richard Bernstein argue that deconstruction does not entail a stylization of the extraordinary that supplants problem solving language with poetic fancy.[53] However, what it does do is call such apparently fixed divisions into question.[54] For this reason it radically contrasts with

Habermas' approach which "involves the kind of typecast binary thinking," as Norris puts it, "that refuses to see how a 'literary' text—or one which exploits a wide range of stylistic resources—might yet possess sufficient *argumentative* force to unsettle deep laid assumptions."[55] This "refusal" on Habermas' part boils down to a rational anxiety over the prospect of "intellectual and moral chaos, radical scepticism, and self-defeating relativism."[56] However, below his effort to oppose such a grim prospect swells a return of the repressed wary of an incipient objectivism with emancipatory effects save that of human happiness; a regulatory ideal that totalises itself; a differentiated dialogue that obscures heterogeneity; a discourse ethic that devitalizes the ethical. It is for these reasons, I hold, that Habermas unexpectedly tries to broach the eccentricity of the religious when he writes that

> I do not believe that we, as Europeans, can seriously understand concepts like morality and ethical life, person and individuality, or freedom and emancipation, without appropriating the substance of the Judeo-Christian understanding of history in terms of salvation ... [W]ithout the...transformation through philosophy of *any one* of the great world religions, this semantic potential could one day become inaccessible. If the remnant of the intersubjectivily shared self-understanding that makes human(e) intercourse possible is not to disintegrate, this potential must be mastered anew by every generation. Each must be able to recognize him - or herself in all that wears a human face. To keep this sense of humanity alive and to clarify it...is certainly a task from which philosophers should not feel themselves wholly excused...[57]

It would be wrong to conclude from this passage that Habermas has taken some sort of "religious turn" in his work. But whatever the contradiction with the basic thrust of his project, it doesn't change the fact that he here expresses a prophetic issue and problematic. The issue concerns the imperative for a more compassionate society; the problematic focuses on the articulation of a religiously informed social ethic suitably fitted to combat the forces of reification. With these aims in mind, Habermas affirms the necessity of philosophically transforming the semantic content of "any one of the great world religions" as a minimum requirement for the moral reform of society. However, the problem with the notion of "philosophical transformation" as Habermas uses it, is its supposition of a neutral set of universal terms servicing a meta-discourse in which dissimilar languages and social worlds are made commensurable without remainder. However, isn't this deflating tactic intrinsic to the very thing that compels Habermas to expound his religio-ethical problematic in the first place: namely, an incipient objectivism with emancipatory effects save that of human happiness; a regulatory ideal that totalises itself; a differentiated dialogue that obscures heterogeneity; a discourse ethic that devitalizes the ethical?

The Transgressive Transformation of Habermas

In order to adequately redress the issue and problematic of a more compassionate society; or in order to develop that "remnant of [an] intersubjectivily shared self-understanding that makes human(e) intercourse possible," it is experimentally advantageous to juxtapose an alternative tradition of thought that extends different ideals beyond Habermas' conclusions, promoting "the possibility of no longer being, doing, or thinking" what Habermas believes "we are, do, and think." Toward this end, I intend to explore the moral-existential framework of religious meaning articulated by Emmanuel Levinas. Following up some of the central themes in his work, it is clear that the religio-ethical motive that Habermas features cannot be had via a philosophical transformation of the religious without remainder. It cannot because the religio-ethical, in its foundational configuration as it were, stands outside of and against the meta-discourse that Habermas assumes so as to render the religio-ethical commensurate to rational philosophy. This "ontology of presence" or "ontology of sameness," as Levinas describes the stance,[58] weakens ethical responsibility by casting our elemental "response-ability" in the shape of a sovereign figure. As a solitary character, this figure meets the human Other (*l'auturi*) as an extension of the Self-as-presence whose first gesture, the gesture of Ego's unrestricted freedom, is to neutralize the otherness of the Other by reducing it to a re-presentation of the disengaged, controlling Subject. Thus, the Self-as-presence denotes a form of subjectivity enslaved by the "dialectic of Enlightenment": a being preoccupied with the sheer struggle to be, with the fate of its own existence, not with that of the Other's.[59]

In radical contrast to this "way-of-being-in-the-world," Levinas pursues a *me*ontological account of moral consciousness as the key to "keeping the religious sense of humanity alive." As the philosopher explains, a meontological approach affirms "a primary mode of non-being (*me-on*)"[60] in which the ethical relation profiles a bond beyond the sheer struggle to be, or that which is "otherwise than being."[61] It is so, Levinas indicates, because the root moment of the ethical surfaces with the nearing of a distinct though unprotected Other whose "face" exposes a summons for incessant vigilance, solicitude, and love. The capacity to hear or heed such a summons is not first conditioned by an ability "to recognize oneself in all that wears a human face," as Habermas put it above. Rather, it is first conditioned by an ethically prior exaction of one's very responsiveness by and through the face of the Other. Says Levinas:

> To expose myself to the vulnerability of the face is to put my ontological right to existence into question. In ethics, the other's right to exist has primacy over my own, a primacy epitomized in the ethical edict: you shall not kill, you shall not jeopardize the life of the other. The ethical rapport with the face is asymmetrical in that it subordinates my existence to the other.[62]

What the philosopher is portraying here is the advent of an ethical subjectivity. For in the shapeless form of the Other's call, or in the stilling jolt of the Other's command, the sovereign Subject is overthrown by a moral consciousness made subject *to* the meontological pre-eminence of the Other *over* and *in* the Self. "It is my inescapable and incontrovertible answerability to the other that makes me an individual 'I'," Levinas contends, "So that I become ... [an] ethical 'I' to the extent that I agree to...dethrone myself—to abdicate my position of centrality—in favour of the vulnerable other."[63] Of course Levinas ultimately maintains that the initiative required to eradicate the Self-as-presence cannot issue from that Self. There can be no superhuman self-overcoming of the Self, as Nietzsche would have it. However, there is the distinct potential for a transcendent or "supernatural" overcoming of the Self insofar that *le surnaturel* evokes a measure of meaning—not Being—over, above, in excess of (*sur*) the natural (*naturel*). It is in keeping with this sense of things that Levinas confirms that "the moral priority of the other over myself could not come to be if it were not motivated by something beyond nature. The ethical situation" he continues to say, "is a human situation beyond human nature, in which the idea of God comes to mind (*Gott fällt mir ein*)."[64] This "idea" emerges here not because the ethical depends on belief but rather the inverse: belief, faith, or trust, depend on the ethical. This is why the philosopher holds that we meet the "holy Other" by being ethically attentive to the human Other.[65] For it is within the ethical relation that "traces of God are to be found,"[66] traces which may very well delineate the "self(less)-understanding" that genuinely "makes human(e) intercourse possible."

The prospect that meaning, individuation, and subjectivity are crucial derivations from the religio-ethical pre-eminence of the Other over the Self constitutes a profound inversion of Habermas' principle method and goal. Whereas he is fiercely determined to promote a rationally motivated consensus as the basis for a universal order of things, Levinas transgressively transforms this ontologically driven need for complete comprehension into a meontologically inspired desire for an irreducible obligation to the Other—whether human or divine—as the epitome of the "human(e)" relationship. What order of things, then, can be derived from this vision of the ethical relationship? What form of critical social theory, for instance, emerges when ethics is the first priority and not ontology or epistemology? Why shouldn't the critical view of social organization be informed by an ethical obligation to the Other over the Self in contrast to mutual understanding and the commensuration of languages, persons, things, and ideas? How can one be so sure that the "God-idea" which "comes to mind" amid the "human situation beyond human nature," is not entirely vital to a profound and truly effective critical social theory that can evade the dialectic of Enlightenment? *Indeed, why not a critical theory of religious insight as a fourth order discourse constructively connected to, though not merely a conduit for, religious sources of meaning?*

Conclusion

With the confrontation of the disparate thought-worlds informing the work of Habermas and Levinas, we have not yet arrived at that final level of discourse. Since Levinas' contribution ultimately embodies a Judaic philosophy of religion—perhaps even a post-Holocaust Judaic philosophy of religion, his work manifests a subtle theological feature making it a point of departure for the moral-existential facet of religious studies rather than an embodiment of its decisive form. This feature is apparent, I believe, in his overly schismatic distinction between the religio-ethical and the ontological that leaves the ontological irreclaimable in a different form. Thus for Levinas, the malevolent struggle to be is deemed irrecusable for the organization of a mass society. In his own words: "Ethics, as the extreme exposure…of one subjectivity to another…hardens its skin as soon as we move into the political world of the impersonal 'third'—the world of government, institutions, tribunals, prisons,…and so on."[67] Consequently "ethics," in contrast to moral ontology, "cannot legislate for society or produce rules of conduct whereby society might be revolutionized or transformed."[68] In effect, the ontological—ethically problematic as it is—can neither be evaded nor reformed. The question that emerges here is; does this distinction, mounting to an irreparable dualism between the spiritual and the material, serve to shield religious faith from argumentative doubt? Yet whether this be the case or no, the result is the same: the value of the ethical as that which is otherwise than being is deflated and weakened by Levinas' subsequent affirmation of an ontological realm that cannot be transformed by the ethical. The task of thinking through this transformation as the transgressive transformation of Levinas, is a labour that undoubtedly presents itself to the scholar of religion: one, perhaps, engaged in the moral-existential facet of religious studies.

Notes

1. Craig Calhoun, *Critical Social Theory: Culture, History, and the Challenge of Difference* (Oxford: Blackwell, 1995), 8.
2. Ibid., 2.
3. At the close of his book, *The Irony of Theology and the Nature of Religious Thought* (Kingston and Montréal: McGill-Queen's University Press, 1991), Wiebe asserts that while religious thought is "directed towards structuring human existence" and thus concerned with the generation of substantial "meaning" (212), scientific thought—and presumably the type of thought associated with the scientific study of religion—"is not concerned with meaning in the [religious] sense at all…" (213) It is rather defined by "a new intention 'to know for the sake of knowing.' Thought now becomes differentiated in a peculiar way and gives rise to a set of beliefs that are wholly cognitive and therefore unconcerned with the social, moral, and political meaning of society. Not only are such beliefs not concerned with structuring a meaningful world picture that determines the obligations of its members," continues Wiebe, "they require a 'diplomatic immunity' from those beliefs that are part of a normative structure" (213). While Wiebe's asocial/amoral/apolitical ethic for scientific production obviously stands in complete opposition to the one I am endeavouring to sketch in this essay, I cannot respond to it at this time. However, given both the positive and negative impact of Wiebe's proposal upon the meaning of religious studies in Canada, it certainly necessitates an informed rejoinder. Toward this end, see P. Travis Kroeker, "The Ironic Cage of Positivism and the Nature of Philosophical Theology," *Studies in Religion/Sciences Religieuses* 22 (1993): 93–103. For Donald Wiebe's response see, "Argument or Authority in the Academy? On Kroeker on *The Irony of Theology*," *Studies in Religion/Sciences Religieuses* 23 (1994): 67–79; and in the same issue, see Kroeker's "Reply to Donald Wiebe," 81–82.
4. Charles Davis, "The Reconvergence of Theology and Religious Studies," *Studies in Religion/Sciences Religieuses* 4 (1974-75): 205–221. See the series of responses to Davis' proposal by Gregory Baum and others in the same volume, 222–236. Also see Donald Wiebe's essay, "The Failure of Nerve in the Academic Study of Religion," *Studies in Religion/Sciences Religieuses* 13 (1984): 401–422, which sparked yet another round of disputation with Davis. For a helpful overview and critical assessment of the Davis-Wiebe debate, see Lorne Dawson's essay, "Neither Nerve nor Ecstasy: Comment on the Wiebe-Davis Ex-

change," *Studies in Religion/Sciences Religieuses* 15 (1986): 145–151.
5. Davis, "The Reconvergence of Theology and Religious Studies," 216.
6. Charles Davis, "Wherein there is No Ecstasy," *Studies in Religion/Sciences Religieuses* 13 (1984): 394.
7. Charles Davis, "The Immanence of Knowledge and the Ecstasy of Faith," *Studies in Religion/Sciences Religieuses* 15 (1986): 195.
8. Thomas E. Helm, *The Christian Religion: An Introduction* (Englewood Cliffs, NJ: Prentice Hall, 1991), xi.
9. Viktor E. Frankl, *Man's Search for Meaning: An Introduction to Logotherapy*, trans. Ilse Lasch (New York: Washington Square Press, 1959), 121–122.
10. Robert Spivey, "Modest Messiahs: The Study of Religion in State Universities," *Religious Education* 63 (1968): 9.
11. For an early though highly influential expression of this concern see Paul Tillich, *The Courage to Be* (London: Collins, 1952).
12. Charles Taylor, *Sources of the Self: The Making of the Modern Identity* (Cambridge, Mass.: Harvard University Press, 1989), 3–24.
13. Ibid., 18.
14. Harold Remus, William Closson James, and Daniel Fraikin, *Religious Studies in Ontario: A State-of-the-Art Review* (Waterloo, Ontario: Wilfrid Laurier University Press, 1992), 295.
15. Max Horkheimer and Theodor Adorno, *Dialectic of Enlightenment*, trans. John Cumming (New York: Continuum, 1990), 12.
16. Jürgen Habermas, *The Philosophical Discourse of Modernity: Twelve Lectures*, trans. Frederick G. Lawrence (Cambridge, Mass.: MIT Press, 1987), 106.
17. Jürgen Habermas, *The New Conservatism: Cultural Criticism and the Historians' Debate*, trans. Shierry Weber Nicholson (Cambridge, Mass.: MIT Press, 1989), 51.
18. Calhoun, *Critical Social Theory*, 44–46, 51.
19. Ibid., 9.
20. Michel Foucault, "What is Enlightenment?" trans. Robert Hurley and others, in *Ethics: Subjectivity and Truth*, vol. 1 of *The Essential Works of Michel Foucault, 1954–1984*, ed. Paul Rabinow (New York: The New Press, 1997), 303–319.
21. Ibid., 309.
22. Ibid., 312, 319.
23. Ibid., 312.
24. Ibid., 315. The final line could also read, "the form of a possible *transgression*" as it does in the translation offered in Paul Rabinow ed., *The Foucault Reader* (New York: Pantheon Books, 1984), 45.
25. Ibid.
26. Ibid., 316.
27. Ibid., 315–316, italics added.
28. See Taylor, *Sources of the Self*.
29. Cf. John Milbank, *Theology and Social Theory: Beyond Secular Reason* (Oxford: Basil Blackwell, 1990). For a critique of Milbank's anti-pluralist proposal for social theory based on a Christian theological metanarrative, see my book, *Critical Theology and the Challenge*

of Jürgen Habermas: Toward a Critical Theory of Religious Insight (New York: Peter Lang, 1999).
30. Emmanuel Levinas and Richard Kearney, "Dialogue with Emmanuel Levinas," in *Face to Face with Levinas*, ed. Richard A. Cohen (Albany, NY: SUNY Press, 1986), 23.
31. Foucault, "What is Enlightenment?" 316.
32. Max Horkheimer, "On the Problem of Truth," in *Between Philosophy and the Social Sciences: Selected Early Writings*, trans. G. Frederick Hunter, Matthew S. Kramer, and John Torpey (Cambridge, Mass.: MIT Press, 1993), 191.
33. Cf. John C. Meagher, *The Truing of Christianity: Visions of Life and Thought for the Future* (New York: Doubleday, 1990).
34. Jürgen Habermas, *Philosophical-Political Profiles*, trans. Frederick G. Lawrence (Cambridge, Mass.: MIT Press, 1983), 12.
35. Jürgen Habermas, "Transcendence from Within, Transcendence in this World," in *Habermas, Modernity and Public Theology*, eds. Don S. Browning and Francis Schüssler Fiorenza (New York: Crossroad, 1992), 227.
36. Jürgen Habermas, *Postmetaphysical Thinking: Philosophical Essays*, trans. Mark Hohengarten (Cambridge, Mass.: MIT Press, 1992), 51. Italics added.
37. Habermas, *The Philosophical Discourse of Modernity*, 309.
38. Ibid., 83.
39. Ibid., 306.
40. Ibid., 93–94.
41. Ibid., 310.
42. Ibid., 187.
43. Ibid., 205.
44. Ibid., 164–165, 178–179, 180–181, 190–191.
45. Habermas, *Postmetaphysical Thinking*, 216.
46. Habermas, *The Philosophical Discourse of Modernity*, 182.
47. Ibid., 164.
48. Ibid., 183.
49. Ibid., 184.
50. Ibid., 309.
51. For some insightful criticisms of Habermas' reading of deconstructionism and postmodern thought in general, see John Rajchman, "Habermas' Complaint," *New German Critique* no. 45 (Winter 1988): 103–114, and Rudi Visker, "Habermas on Heidegger and Foucault: Meaning and Validity in *The Philosophical Discourse of Modernity*," *Radical Philosophy* 61 (Summer 1992): 15–22.
52. Christopher Norris, "Deconstruction, Postmodernism and Philosophy: Habermas on Derrida," in *Derrida: A Critical Reader*, ed. David Wood (Oxford: Basil Blackwell, 1992), 182.
53. Ibid., 184. Also see Richard Bernstein, *The New Constellation: The Ethical-Political Horizons of Modernity/Postmodernity* (Cambridge, Mass.: MIT Press, 1991), 221.
54. Norris, "Deconstruction, Postmodernism and Philosophy," 184.
55. Ibid., 190.

56. Bernstein, *The New Constellation*, 17.
57. Habermas, *Postmetaphysical Thinking*, 15.
58. Levinas and Kearney, "Dialogue with Emmanuel Levinas," 19, 24.
59. Ibid., 26.
60. Ibid., 25.
61. Cf. Emmanuel Levinas, *Otherwise Than Being: Or, Beyond Essence*, trans. Alphonso Lingis (The Hague: Martinus Nijhoff, 1981).
62. Levinas and Kearney, "Dialogue with Emmanuel Levinas," 24.
63. Ibid., 27.
64. Ibid., 25.
65. Ibid., 23.
66. Ibid., 31.
67. Ibid., 30–31.
68. Ibid., 29.

Essay Four

Fragments of Religion:
An Exercise in Critical Post-Religious Thought

WHAT IS the meaning and purpose of religious thought today?

Beyond the circle and community of faith, the importance or urgency of this question may not be immediately evident. Since modern western secular thought tends to deflate or even undermine religious claims to truth or validity, they cannot but seem illusory.[1] It is difficult to underestimate the impact of this secular problematization of religion. At the most basic level, it has meant the diminution of the very richness and openness of human experience as religious events are dismissed as epiphenomena. At a more complex level, it has meant the need to continually debate and defend—either explicitly or implicitly—the elementary worth of one's religious discourse *as* religious. *How can this strain not impede genuine theoretical growth or breakthrough?* Granted, contemporary approaches to the study of religion have moved beyond the modern penchant to explain away the religious as fanciful all the way down. In contrast to this crude reductionism, current social scientific and philosophical methods focus on the historical particularity of all religious traditions in relation to wider socio-cultural trends and developments. Here the task is to accurately describe, sufficiently explain, and appropriately understand how religion (in its many facets) interacts with its surrounding environment.[2] Still, this strategy does not quite transcend the secular ethos that informs modern western culture as a whole. Indeed, many would conclude that it simply confirms the bias: for religion is here examined as a characteristic *human* activity, and seldom as anything *more*.[3]

While this essay is *not* prepared to argue that the gravity of contemporary religious thought requires a supernatural intervention that annuls or ignores the secular challenge,[4] *neither* is it prepared to designate this peculiar "more" as a purely private affair. Sensing the pull of a lingering religiosity that remains culturally profound, *the following interpretation attempts to chart the upsurge of an unforced theological moment in creative relation to a religious thinking with critical consequences.*[5] This is to say, that the meaning and purpose of religious thought today may be re-animated by following up the contingent circulation of fragmented religious contents that *as religious* and *as fragmented* motion toward the critical transgression of what we have become.[6]

Somewhat paradoxically, perhaps, this project reveals a certain "post-religious" inspiration. By "post-religious" I do not mean the erasure of religious language, thought, experience, or institutions from the fund of extant meaning that shapes human existence.[7] Rather I intend the secular segmentation and curtailment of religious worldviews and the concomitant recognition and experience of diverse religious traditions. Religious culture, in this context, is always a sub-culture, but one with multiple fronts that are stretched and pulled in numerous directions. Under this pressure, religious contents tend to overflow their traditional containers into ever wider forms of non-religious discourse, surfacing, from time to time, as an awkward idea, an out of place theme, a curious expression, or a repressed supposition. It is at this juncture that the critical religious thinker can cultivate such "fragments of religion" so as to "deterritorialize"[8] the established conceptual landscape; disrupt prevailing ways of thinking and speaking; show up the limits of thought as concealed by its familiarity; and intimate the way beyond such conventionality by constructively envisioning *what we might yet be*.[9]

Thus, the drive and direction of a critical post-religious thinking forwards its own unique promise. By way of outlining the historical, socio-cultural, and philosophical framework that may account for this promise, and by way of exploring its potential application, the following essay inspects "The Rise and Range of the Religious Fragment Today," and "The Insurgent Fragment of Religious Love in Albert Camus' *The Rebel*." While the effort in the first section is dedicated to a *dialectical analysis* of the religious fragment in relationship to tradition as played out within modernity, the second section is devoted to an examination of Camus' notion of "strange love" as a religious fragment with critical implications for "exclusive humanism."[10] Taken together, both sections make manifest some of the structures and details of "A Critical Post-religious Thinking" which concludes the essay. It is here where the meaning and purpose of religious thought today may come to light.

The Rise and Range of the Religious Fragment Today

"Tradition," notes Vladimir Lossky, "is one of those terms which, through being too rich in meanings, runs the risk of finally having none."[11] In other words, the coherence of "Tradition" must signify a rule of faith that can set clear boundaries to what can count as "Christian," "Orthodox," "Catholic," or what have you. Beyond these boundaries, all "hell" breaks loose. However, what is troublesome for the Orthodox theologian may prove to be a boon for the "postorthodox" religious thinker.[12] The excess of meaning that Lossky laments may actually disclose the unaffected extension of traditional religious contents to unconventional yet *concurrent* contexts. Indeed, the import and character of this extension may yet signify another "rule"—though one that problematizes rather than assuring a rigid measure of things.

Consider the work of Wilfred Cantwell Smith.[13] As he sees it, religious traditions constitute an historical repository of the engagement of things thought divine. Over the centuries, there is an accumulation of these encounters forming a "mixed pool of elements" (to borrow Benson Saler's characterization[14]) in which some of these elements are transmitted, some are transformed, some are augmented, and some are simply forgotten. The total form and substance of any one religious tradition is therefore unavailable for singular representation. At most or even at best, there exists a limited range of the total tradition that is open to a selective appropriation.[15] Yet it is this very process of selection that helps to generate a plurality of traditions and sub-traditions among each of the world religions, giving voice to a polyphonic discourse rather than some neatly contained, monologic soliloquy. *Fragmentation is thus part and parcel of the dynamics of tradition as such.*

Examining the matter historically rather than dogmatically, Smith's analysis is materially obvious. Still, his insights may appear odd to religious adherents who continue to claim a distinctive "Tradition" as their own rather than some variable set of religious doctrines, beliefs, or practices. For isn't there a form of religious appropriation that is far more concerned to ground a substantial identity in relation to a secured "Tradition" rather than a differentiated, "post-conventional" religious consciousness?[16] And isn't Smith's approach indicative of the contemporary disdain for religious (or moral) normalization as the very antithesis of true individuality, autonomy, creativity, and freedom?

We have to answer positively here. However, this affirmation does not automatically imply that Smith's approach is biased, misleading, or distorting. *It suggests that significant historical shifts in cultural sensibility will generate a different range of experience and insight that ultimately yields a changed object domain.* Thus, what comes into view as an "object" for analysis; or what appears or shows itself for further study, is *not* completely detached from the type or form of interpretation that, dialectically, contours the very manifestation and reality of the object itself. It is important to recognize that this shaping cannot be explained as the imposition of a transformed consciousness upon an otherwise fixed or stable object. As Charles Taylor points out, to modify our understanding and description of things is to effect their transfiguration at the level of meaning and, in turn, to influence what can count as "good" or "bad" content, or "true" or "false" representation, etc.[17] To conclude the point, the experience and reality of that which we tend to designate "religious tradition" will depend, in part, upon the kind of designation at work. Smith's version of the development and meaning of religion, then, anticipates its dialectical configuration under contemporary conditions of life and thought.

To cultivate a religious thinking with critical consequences is, in some sense, to begin here. One point of departure (and the secret of Smith's inspiration, I believe) is to recognize and work with the assorted viewpoints that adhere to any religious tradition. Such "heteroglossia"—to borrow Mikhail Bakhtin's term[18]—not only makes manifest the linguistic richness and conceptual depth of most traditions, but ultimately denotes an open-ended quality that resists the conservative drift toward sheer traditionalism. As Michael Gardiner explains the matter:

> the historicity of tradition ensures that a given interpretation can never be complete or infallible, insofar as tradition is the mode through which our understanding of the world evolves and is expressed. Each succeeding historical epoch embodies new experiences and perspectives; each period interprets past texts in different and novel ways. Thus, meaning is 'open,' incomplete, in a continual state of becoming.[19]

The constant struggle for meaning featured by this portrayal cannot but engender a conspicuous degree of uncertainty. However for the contemporary mindset, such ambivalence can encourage spirited exploration just as much as it does anxiety. The utter plurality and ambiguity that animates historical existence, then, may not imply a muddled diversity in need of a stricter uniformity, but rather a spectrum of untried possibilities in need of an adventurous spirit.

That such a spirit exists is, according to Craig Calhoun and Werner Marx, most evident. Human beings hardly ever live out their days within a singular horizon of meaning to the rigid exclusion of other perspectives. (Says Montaigne, "No generous spirit stays within itself...Its pursuits have no bounds or rules; its food is wonder, search, and ambiguity."[20]) While the modern rationalist assumption insists that "normal," fully functional human beings can only efficiently manage a uniform order of things, the contemporary emphasis accents our concurrent embrace of manifold, often contradictory, viewpoints. Calhoun maintains that human beings simultaneously inhabit "multiple social worlds,"[21] continually shifting between widely divergent, albeit, historically grounded outlooks. What this activity yields is a porous understanding of self, others, and world in which human being and meaning are literally "com-plex." It is perhaps for this reason that Smith asserts that "There is no ideal faith that I ought to have."[22] Indeed, "I would recognize," says Smith, "that any one man's faith is different any given morning from what it was the proceeding afternoon."[23] Yet far from intimating the disintegration of meaning as such, the capacity to move from one social world to another may actually disclose the human aptitude for intellectual, emotional, and spiritual growth.[24] So, "Instead of complaining about the *fragmentation* of our relation to the world today," writes Werner Marx, we should "stop and be amazed by the fact that our…understanding…apparently moves with ease and as a matter of course in many everyday worlds simultaneously and consecutively and that, in doing so, *it is in no way confronted with chaos…* "[25]

While these last thoughts have a noticeable "postmodern" ring to them, the focus upon plurality, ambiguity, multiplicity, and fragmentation represents a fairly modern concern.[26] It is *aesthetic modernism* that obtains a distinct resonance here. Against the triumph of positivism and the decay of religious faith that unfolded during the late 19th and early 20th centuries,[27] modernist art, music, literature, and philosophy explored "the paradoxical many-sidedness of the world. Alarmed at the spectre of nihilism, the loss of meaning in transcendent imperatives and firm secular values," observes Eugene Lunn, modernists saw "reality as necessarily constructed from relative perspectives, while they [sought] to exploit the aesthetic and ethical richness of ambiguous images, sounds, and authorial points of view."[28] Or to cite André Guide, art becomes an "'exploitation of an uncertainty.'"[29]

With the sounding of these particular themes, our dialectical design pushes us to consider whether the celebration of uncertainty might help to obscure the true nature of social reality. To what degree does the valuation of plurality, multiplicity, ambiguity, and fragmentation paralyse rational analysis or ideology-critique by foisting the present situation upon the human subject as a species of blind fate?[30] The polyphonic array of things both past or present is a phenomena that may only come to light within the capitalist epoch, for instance.[31] The conflictual character of its individualistic ethic tends to divide, separate, and disjoin community so as to facilitate the boundless accumulation of private property.[32] With the development of the consumerist ethos, this tendency intensifies to the point of concocting a "hyper-phonic" simulacrum of recycled signs, sounds, images, slogans, messages, and texts where genuine insight is sacrificed to the capricious liberty of arbitrary information.[33] Without lapsing into an essentialism here, we can still wonder how any claim that exalts sheer fragmentation can evade the barren prospect that "anything goes."

In a certain sense it can't nor should it: effective critique cannot be ventured from some point outside of our historical, social, or cultural situation.[34] Yet this specific situation is not devoid of its own fissures or gaps. The clash of social worlds wrought by the pressure of capitalism and consumerism doesn't always collapse the distinctiveness of particularity into an undifferentiated store of amorphous expressions. At times, the friction of their juxtaposition displays a critical singularity that stands in opposition to the uncritical whole.[35] It is for this reason that the modern attitude evinces a growing awareness of non-identity and otherness—of that which escapes totality. What this "exit"[36] insinuates is that the all-encompassing "whole" is no longer inviolate. Nor are its typical accomplices: metaphysics, the *apriori*, universal reason or morality, religious faith.[37] Fleeing these options, the modern work of thought arises and arrives in a fragmented form, creating an interruption that promises fresh insight.[38] However, more than a breakthrough in understanding is signalled here. The discernment of otherness and the non-identical also conveys an ethical concern insofar that it latches on to the discarded or forgotten facets of the "damaged life" (*Adorno*) as that which stands outside of and against the normative order, darkly illuminating its inability to exhaust the meaning of things. Yet with this negation arises the constructive task of rendering justice to the most marginalized, most vulnerable members of an overly complicated, often harsh social order. Interestingly enough, it is precisely this challenge that animates the work of Albert Camus.

The Insurgent Fragment of Religious Love in Albert Camus' *The Rebel*

By way of demonstrating the critical import of the "rise and range of the religious fragment today, " I would like to take up an examination of *The Rebel*[39] by the philosopher-novelist, Albert Camus. Responding to the communist and capitalist alternatives bearing down upon post-War Europe; reflecting upon the uses and abuses of history within politics, philosophy, and religion; concerned to flesh out the role of the engaged artist in our time; and morally driven to comprehend how and why the early 20th century managed to devastate millions of lives, *The Rebel* recommends itself for our analysis on numerous fronts. However, the most germane carves out the following problematic: "Is it possible to find a rule of conduct outside the realm of religion and its absolute values?"[40] Camus' *affirmative* answer to this question advances a compelling correlation between resistance to injustice, the significance of love, and the prospect of rebellion, all in the wake of the death of God.[41] Nevertheless, it is precisely within this complex of issues that we can discern the course of a religious fragment that emerges to unsettle Camus' discourse while simultaneously pressing religious thought in unique directions. In other words, *The Rebel* evinces the *upsurge of an unforced theological moment in creative relation to a religious thinking with critical consequences.*

Rebellion, according to Camus, entails saying "No" to injustice and oppression; of refusing to be treated as a mere object.[42] This refusal cannot be entirely explained as sheer renunciation, however. For concealed within the initial negation resides a double affirmation: a saying "Yes" to justice, freedom, and equality, on the one hand; and a saying "Yes" to the risk of shaping the world according to these values, on the other.[43] Writes Camus: "[I]n every act of rebellion, the rebel simultaneously experiences a feeling of revulsion at the infringement of his rights and a complete and spontaneous loyalty to certain aspects of himself. Thus he implicitly brings into play a standard of values so far from being gratuitous that he is prepared to support it no matter what the risks."[44] Rooted in, what we could call, an "exclusive humanism,"[45] Camus still contends that rebellion is a non-egotistic act.[46] It is so because the spurning of injustice not only spontaneously arises among the subjugated, but also mounts among sensitive witnesses to oppression who rebel against injustice done to others.[47] For these witnesses, "suffering is seen as a collective experience."[48] Rebellion is therefore a gesture that draws people out of and beyond themselves: it is, for Camus, a notable form of *humane transcendence*.

Of course Camus endeavours to differentiate such transcendence from its religious type. "The rebel is a man," Camus remarks, "who is on the point of accepting or rejecting the sacred and determined on laying claim to a human situation in which the answers are human—in other words, formulated in reasonable terms. From this moment every question, every word, is an act of rebellion while in the sacred world every word is an act of grace."[49] This is to say, if one sides with the sacred rather than rebellion, then one must perceive and accept the totality of existence as coming from God, as part and parcel of his self-communication to the world. Thus the realities of injustice, suffering, and oppression embody a mysterious purpose within the salvific scheme of things which requires belief.[50] "But suffering exhausts hope and faith and then is left alone and unexplained," counters Camus. "The toiling masses, worn out with suffering and death are masses without God."[51] So Camus—certainly no stranger to misery[52]—concludes we are living in an "unsacrosanct moment in history."[53] It is, therefore, the time of the rebel. However, can rebellion by itself reveal a realm of values and a form of transcendence that are completely "unsacrosanct" or devoid of all religious connotations? Or how truly exclusive is this humanism?

As a movement away from the solitude of self and world and toward the other human being in need, rebellion insinuates an excessiveness that Camus characterizes as "*un étrange amour*"[54]—"a strange love." As he emphatically puts it, "*rebellion cannot exist without a strange form of love.*"[55] So what exactly does he mean by this? And why can't rebellion exist without it? "Strange love," Camus suggests, is a type of love that empties itself for the sake of the suffering Other; a love that freely gives itself away to the good fight against injustice, tyranny, and persecution; a distinct selfless love that is, nevertheless, grounded in the realities of *this* world. As he clarifies, "its merit lies in making no calculations, distributing everything it posses to life and living men [*à ses frères vivants*]."[56] Those who live by and through such a love gladly throw in their lot with the damned, the wretched, and the humiliated, knowingly rejecting all forms of salvation in sudden solidarity with those who lie beyond the pale of such redemption.[57] This "path of sympathy," as Camus calls it elsewhere,[58] is "the very movement of love itself."[59] Yet it is also *the very movement of its strangeness* as it presses beyond the self-serving or expedient reaction to the impingement of the Other by granting her or him ethical priority over the selfsame.[60] In this sense, strange love is inherently inordinate, uncanny, disturbing—rebellious. Thus, rebellion "is love…or it is nothing at all."[61]

Yet, despite these profound and fervent avowals of love for—dare we say it?—"the neighbour," Camus never entirely explains nor justifies its foundational role. As he insinuates, "man's love [*passion*] for man can be born of other things than…a theoretical confidence in human nature."[62] That reply, however, is too easy.[63] For if it is indeed the case that "rebellion cannot exist without a strange form of love," then Camus' position requires that the full weight of that love be *unpacked in different ways* lest its full import be obscured or lost.

Toward that end, we might begin by noting that a love freely extended to the stranger without expectation of return places it on the far side of things thought "reasonable."[64] "Reasonable," in this case, might rather understand social responsibility in contractual terms as an agreement to accept reciprocal obligations that ensure the mutuality of social life. Yet as Emmanuel Levinas has observed, "The biological human brotherhood—conceived with the sober coldness of Cain—is not a sufficient reason from me to be responsible for a separated being."[65] Otherwise put, true human fellowship doesn't occur because we are all thought to share the exact same set of needs and interests that can be easily quantified, measured, equated, and exchanged. No, genuine sociality is neither so materially nor rationally obvious. What is obvious, thinks Camus, is a requisite love that remains outside of or exterior to individual or collective dispensation. This is to say, the kind of love deemed central to rebellion is wholly *gratuitous*—Camus' demurrals notwithstanding.[66] Indeed, strange love is something that arises from beyond us; a kind of love that one shares in and conveys to others but which resists manipulation and control. The *transcendent* character of this love, then, cannot but clash with its assertion as an *unalloyed* humane inclination or value. On the contrary, "strange love" evokes something beyond human nature; something otherwise than being; something completely eccentric; something wholly other. *Thus, the idea of God comes to mind.*[67]

With that idea in play, the notion of strange love is clarified as the theological moment ascends with the exploration of its religious fragment to append a distinct *conceptual*, *linguistic*, and *moral* level of meaning that critically expands—at the level of analysis—Camus' proposal. For as an echo of God's freely given love to humankind, "strange love" constitutes a transformative force. It does so because, as gratuitous, it is not strictly ours to give nor keep but is rather meant to radiate outward, entailing a resolute leaving of Self (a form of leaving, we might add, first envisioned as God's creation of the world; a leaving further shaped as Revelation; and a leaving radicalized as *kenosis*— "[for] although He existed in the form of God, [He] did not regard equality with God a thing to be grasped, but emptied Himself, taking the form of a bond-servant, and being made in the likeness of men" [Philippians 2:6–7]). As a result, religious love does not await the manifestation of some acceptable level of loveableness before taking action, *but goes out to create such loveableness where it does not yet exist.*[68] "Only thus will we break the cycle of injury and vengeance," perceives Charles Davis, "only thus will we call a halt to the cumulative effect of hatred responding to hatred."[69] Or only thus will we be able to continually redress the ongoing "plague" of injustice.[70] Says Levinas, "God rises to his supreme and ultimate presence as correlative to the justice rendered unto men."[71] To be sure, this is not the impassable God that Camus declares dead. More to the point, it is the "persecuted God of the prophets"[72]; the loving and compassionate God of Jesus Christ; and the God exhumed from *The Rebel* by creatively pursuing its fragment of religion as an unforced theological moment with critical consequences.

Conclusion

For those familiar with the work and criticism of Albert Camus, the above analysis may not seem very original. Many have claimed a Christian inspiration to Camus' literature and philosophy, regardless of his elusive comments on the issue. To be sure, Camus' reflections may very well bear witness to the pull of a lingering religiosity that remains culturally profound. It therefore deserves to be explored in a variety of ways if we are to fully understand both the artist and the philosopher. Thus, this study has nothing to excuse nor lament. At the same time, though, it would be a mistake to confuse Camus' religiosity with a firm theological position or faith. It is highly problematic, I believe, to endeavour to "prove" that the "host" discourse is somehow always already religious, or always already theological, or always already Christian. Such an imputation can only serve to elide the fragments of religion that have seeped into Camus' humanism as exclusive rather than as religious. Thus, the fragments of religion hold up as fragments, while their theological moment—*as a moment*—crystallizes in relation to the critical operation of a post-religious thinking intent on transgression.

Toward that end, I hold that my analysis of *The Rebel* demonstrates a distinct limit to "exclusive humanism." Here the religious content surfaces to disturb the ideal of a humanism that allows no escape from ourselves as finite human beings; a humanism which is thought to be exhausted by its this-worldly framework and reference; or a humanism where the only details that matter are those things which sustain life "here and now." Anything peripheral to that particular focus just isn't perceived. This is not to suggest a new or refurbished metaphysics as an adequate alternative. It is simply to press the fragments of religion up against cherished suppositions that are embraced without serious questioning or debate. For this reason, as Charles Taylor has noted, "To speak of aiming beyond life is to appear to undermine the supreme concern with life of our humanitarian, 'civilized' world."[73] Well, maybe it does. In the case of "strange love," its disruption involves the embellishment of its religious reverberations. What this suggests is that an excessive love—strange or not—is possible "only to the extent that we open ourselves to God, which means, in fact, overstepping the limits set in theory by exclusive humanism."[74] Thus, the transgressive transformation of "strange love" involves the effort to see this love as related to a God who, beyond humanism, opens up the prospect of truly loving the Other in a novel way.

Fundamental to this "way," I would also argue, is the history, particularity, character, and reference of religious language as such. This is said not only to deflect the usual secular rejection of religious terms as beside the point; nor is it advanced only to bolster the prospect of a religious rhetoric of disruption, however pertinent that may be. No, the principal concern centres upon the value of *substantial* moral, ontological, and epistemological terms necessary for the development of a thorough critical vision of things. For such substance shapes the very range of possible thought and experience by allowing for a "mind-full" thematization of what we consider to be of the utmost importance. It matters a great deal, then, to be able to use a term like "love" in an evolving critical discourse, and even more vital still, I believe, to take up phrases such as "God's love," or the "gratuitous love of God." If it is indeed the case, as Taylor has strongly submitted, that "We find the sense of life through articulating it," by "framing meaningful expressions which are adequate,"[75] then religious language must hold as religious. Stepping beyond the boundaries of exclusive humanism, the centrality of religious language steps up to make its contribution to the post-religious quest for meaning.

So, what is the meaning and purpose of religious thought today?

In view of the dynamics of tradition within a modern cultural context and secular society; in view of the fragments of religion become "nomadic"[76]; in view of their critical potential to show up the limits of what we have become; and in view of the fact that "meaning is 'open,' incomplete, [and] in a continual state of becoming,"[77] one track open to the religious thinker today is to begin to shape, in substantive religious terms, various ways of being in the world. In this fashion, the religious thinker begins to motion toward what we might yet be. To do so in a form that is adequate to our post-religious situation, though, may demand a critical theory of religious thought. That, however, is the subject for another analysis.

Notes

1. Of course the classic example of this approach to religion is Sigmund Freud's *The Future of an Illusion*, trans. James Strachey (New York: Norton, 1989).
2. Walter H. Capps, *Religious Studies: The Making of a Discipline* (Minneapolis: Fortress

Press, 1995), 1–104.

3. I say "seldom" because even within the social-scientific study of religion, the phenomenological approach as represented by Otto, Shonderblom and Eliade (among others) were concerned to make manifest the ultimate or divine power that generates all religious phenomena. To be sure, this approach to the study of religion constitutes an important part of its historical evolution. Nevertheless, it is a development that has been judged to be highly problematic since it is believed to advance a not so hidden Christian theological agenda. At its most extreme, Donald Wiebe has argued in *The Irony of Theology and the Nature of Religious Thought* (Kingston and Montréal: McGill-Queen's University Press, 1991), that genuine scientific thought—including scientific thought about religion—"is not concerned with meaning in the [religious] sense at all…" (213) There is much to be clarified and sorted out here. For one, to completely bracket theological meaning in the study of religion seems unscientific given the role such meaning plays in the establishment and articulation of the different world religions. For another, it is rather myopic to claim that only Christian scholars have an interest in the meaning, role, and purpose of religious faith. The same can certainly be noted of scholars of Judaism, Islam, Hinduism, the East Asian religions and beyond.

4. This would seem to be the "radical orthodox" strategy championed by John Milbank in *Theology and Social Theory: Beyond Secular Reason* (Oxford: Basil Blackwell, 1990), 206–255.

5. I recognize that these terms are fairly imprecise, though I hold they are not without their own kind of clarity and purpose. Still, the exact nature and character of the "theological moment" is difficult to define. In general terms, my aim is to dodge the evocation of "theology" as a discipline with special suppositions that evade critical inspection, while allowing for the intersection of "theological" ideas, concerns, interests, terms, sentiments etc., that may prove vital to the formation of "other" kinds of discourse. In this case, the theological content must abstain from overwhelming its secular accomplice, while the secular must resist totally absorbing the theological content without remainder. Left hanging in the balance, I believe, is a "theological moment." Obviously, more thinking on this particular issue remains to be carried out.

6. Michel Foucault, "What is Enlightenment?" trans. Robert Hurley and others, in *Ethics: Subjectivity and Truth*, vol. 1 of *The Essential Works of Michel Foucault*, ed. Paul Rabinow (New York: The New Press, 1997), 303–319.

7. Indeed, contemporary western culture is rife with diverse religious activities. See Peter C. Emberly, *Divine Hunger: Canadians on a Spiritual Walkabout* (Toronto: HarperColiins, 2002).

8. Gilles Deleuze, "Nomad Thought," in *The New Nietzsche*, ed. David B. Allison (Cambridge, Mass.: MIT Press, 1985), 144.

9. Craig Calhoun, *Critical Social Theory: Culture, History, and the Challenge of Difference* (Oxford: Blackwell, 1995), xviii, 9.

10. The phrase is Charles Taylor's, though used in a very different context. See his work, *A Catholic Modernity?* (New York: Oxford, 1999).

11. Vladimir Lossky, *In the Image and Likeness of God* (Crestwood, NY: St. Vladimir's

Seminary Press, 1974), 141.
12. On the meaning and intent of this term see essay one in this volume, "From Postmodernity to Postorthodoxy, Or Charles Davis and the Contemporary Context of Christian Thought."
13. Wilfred Cantwell Smith, *The Meaning and End of Religion: A New Approach to the Religious Traditions of Mankind* (New York: Mentor Books, 1964).
14. Benson Saler, *Conceptualizing Religion: Immanent Anthropologists, Transcendent Natives, and Unbounded Categories* (New York: E.J. Brill, 1993), 195–226.
15. Smith, *The Meaning and End of Religion*, 8, 141–145, 152.
16. The terminology is Kohlberg's, though I am borrowing it from the work of Jürgen Habermas, "Moral Development and Ego Identity," in *Communication and the Evolution of Society*, trans. Thomas McCarthy (Boston: Beacon Press, 1979), 69–94. For its application to religious identity see Charles Davis, "Our New Religious Identity," in *Religion and the Making of Society* (Cambridge: Cambridge University Press, 1994), 131–152.
17. Charles Taylor, "Reply and Re-articulation," in *Philosophy in an Age of Pluralism: The Philosophy of Charles Taylor in Question*, ed. James E. Tully (Cambridge: Cambridge University Press, 1994), 221.
18. For more on this concept and the work of Bakhtin, see Michael Gardiner, *The Dialogics of Critique: M.M. Bakhtin and the Theory of Ideology* (London: Routledge, 1992); Michael Holquist, *Dialogism: Bakhtin and his World* (London: Routledge, 1990); and Tzvetan Todorov, *Mikhail Bakhtin: The Dialogical Principle*, trans. Wlad Godzich (Minneapolis: University of Minnesota Press, 1984).
19. Gardiner, *The Dialogics of Critique*, 109.
20. Michel de Montaigne, "On Experience," in *Essays*, trans. J.M. Cohen (London: Penguin, 1958), 348.
21. Calhoun, *Critical Social Theory*, xix.
22. Smith, *The Meaning and End of Religion*, 172.
23. Ibid, 171. This is also perhaps the reason why the 19th century French romanticist Gérard de Nerval could respond to Victor Hugo's charge that Nerval "had no religion" by saying: "You think I have no religion? I have seventeen of them…at least!" For more on Nerval and others of this period see Michel Despland, *Reading an Erased Code: Romantic Religion and Literary Aesthetics in France* (Toronto: University of Toronto Press, 1994), 104.
24. Calhoun, *Critical Social Theory*, xix.
25. Werner Marx, *Towards a Phenomenology of Ethics: Ethos and the Life-World*, trans. Ashraf Noor (Albany, NY: SUNY Press, 1992), 106. Italics added.
26. Or alternatively, we could say that there are certain types of postmodern thought that constitute attenuated forms of aesthetic modernism as both Fredric Jameson and Andreas Huyssen have rightly observed. See Fredric Jameson, "Forward," in Jean-François Lyotard, *The Postmodern Condition: A Report on Knowledge*, trans. Geoff Bennington and Brian Massumi (Minneapolis: University of Minnesota Press, 1984), vii–xxi; and Andreas Huyssen, "Mapping the Postmodern," in *After the Great Divide: Modernism, Mass Culture, Postmodernism* (Bloomington: Indiana University Press, 1986), 179–221.
27. H. Stuart Hughes, "The Decade of the 1880s: The Revolt Against Positivism," in *Consciousness and Society: The Reconstruction of European Social Thought, 1890–1930* (New

York: Vintage, 1961), 33–66.
28. Eugene Lunn, *Marxism and Modernism: An Historical Study of Lukács, Brecht, Benjamin and Adorno* (Berkeley: University of California Press, 1982), 36.
29. Cited in Lunn, *Marxism and Modernism*, 48.
30. See Max Horkheimer, "Traditional and Critical Theory," in *Critical Theory: Selected Essays*, trans. Matthew J. O'Connell and others (New York: Continuum, 1972): "…their work and its results are alienated from them [the workers], and the whole process with all its waste of work-power and human life, and with its wars and its senseless wretchedness, seems to be an unchangeable force of nature, a fate beyond man's control" (204). Also see Horkheimer's "Materialism and Morality," in *Between Philosophy and the Social Sciences: Selected Early Writings*, trans. G. Frederick Hunter, Matthew S. Kramer, and John Torpey (Cambridge, Mass.: MIT Press, 1993), 36.
31. As Mikhail Bakhtin observed in *Problems of Dostoevsky's Poetics*, trans. Caryl Emerson (Minneapolis: University of Minnesota Press, 1984), the birth of the modern "polyphonic novel" could only have been realized

> in the capitalist era. The most favourable soil for it was moreover precisely in Russia, where capitalism set in almost catastrophically, and where it came upon an untouched multitude of diverse worlds and social groups which had not been weakened in their individual isolation, as in the West, by the gradual encroachment of capitalism. Here in Russia the contradictory nature of evolving [capitalist] social life…was bound to appear particularly abrupt, and at the same time the individuality of those worlds, worlds thrown off their ideological balance and colliding with one another, was bound to be particularly full and vivid. In this way the objective preconditions were created for the multi-leveledness and multi-voicedness of the polyphonic novel. (19–20)

32. Horkheimer, "Morality and Materialism," 19.
33. Frederic Jameson, *Postmodernism, Or, The Cultural Logic of Late Capitalism* (Durham: Duke University Press, 1991), 1–54.
34. Horkheimer, "Traditional and Critical Theory."
35. Bakhtin, *Problems of Dostoevsky's Poetics*, 20.
36. Foucault, "What is Enlightenment?" 305.
37. Stephen H. Watson, "On the Rationality of the Fragment," in *Extensions: Essays on Interpretation, Rationality, and the Closure of Modernism* (Albany, NY: SUNY Press, 1992), 248, 251–52.
38. Here the work of Franz Kafka is obviously emblematic. One, of course, could cite the contribution of Nietzsche as well as Max Horkheimer and Theodor Adorno's classic work *Dialektik der Aufklärung: Philosophische Fragmente* (Amsterdam: Querido, 1947).
39. Albert Camus, *The Rebel: An Essay on Man in Revolt*, trans. Anthony Bower (New York: Vintage Books, 1956). The original French version was simply entitled, *L'Homme Révolté* (Paris: Gallimard, 1951). For other commentary on Camus see Lev Braun, *Witness to Decline; Albert Camus: Moralist of the Absurd* (Rutherford, NJ: Fairleigh Dickinson Univer-

sity Press, 1974); Bettina L. Kropp, ed., *Critical Essays on Albert Camus* (Boston: G.K. Hall, 1988); Thomas Merton, *Albert Camus' The Plague* (New York: Seabury Press, 1968); David Sprintzen, *Camus: A Critical Examination* (Philadelphia: Temple University Press, 1988).

40. Camus, *The Rebel*, 21.
41. Ibid., 62.
42. Ibid., 250.
43. Ibid., 13.
44. Ibid., 13–14.
45. Again, recall the phrase belongs to the work of Charles Taylor, *A Catholic Modernity?* 19.
46. Camus, *The Rebel*, 16.
47. Ibid., 16–17.
48. Ibid., 22.
49. Ibid., 21.
50. Such is the theological position of the character Father Paneloux in Camus' novel *The Plague*, trans. Stuart Gilbert (New York: Vintage, 1984). See especially pages 94–99 and 216–234.
51. Camus, *The Rebel*, 303.
52. See Stephen Bronner, *Camus: Portrait of a Moralist* (Minneapolis: University of Minnesota Press, 1999); Patrick McCarthy, *Camus: A Critical Study of His Life and Work* (London: Hamish Hamilton, 1982).
53. Camus, *The Rebel*, 21.
54. Camus, *L'Homme Révolté*, 364.
55. Camus, *The Rebel*, 304. Italics added.
56. Ibid., 304.
57. Ibid., 57.
58. In *The Plague* the character Tarrou explains: "…'I decided to take, in every predicament, the victim's side, so as to reduce the damage done. Among them I can at least try to discover how one attains … peace'" (254).
59. Camus, *L'Homme Révolté*, 32.
60. The ideas are Camus', but the language belongs to the work of the Jewish philosopher, Emmanuel Levinas. See his works *Totality and Infinity: An Essay on Exteriority*, trans. Alphonso Lingis (Pittsburg: Duquesne University Press, 1969); and *Otherwise than Being: Or, Beyond Essence*, trans. Alphonso Lingis (The Hague: Matinus Nijhoff Press, 1981).
61. Camus, *The Rebel*, 304.
62. Ibid., 18.
63. This is more or less the same answer that Max Horkheimer gives in relation to his evocation of love in his essay "Materialism and Morality." For my analysis of Horkheimer on this score, see essay five in this volume, "A Critical Theory of Religious Insight."
64. Camus, *The Rebel*, 21. This is especially the case given that Camus was fully aware of how easily humankind can slip into an incorrigible barbarism.
65. Emmanuel Levinas, "God and Philosophy," in *The Levinas Reader*, ed. Seán Hand (Oxford: Basil Blackwell, 1989), 180.

66. To cite the pertinent passage again from *The Rebel*: "[I]n every act of rebellion, the rebel simultaneously experiences a feeling of revulsion at the infringement of his rights and a complete and spontaneous loyalty to certain aspects of himself. Thus he implicitly brings into play *a standard of values so far from being gratuitous* that he is prepared to support it no matter what the risks" (14). Italics added.
67. See Emmanuel Levinas and Richard Kearney, "Dialogue with Emmanuel Levinas," in *Face to Face with Levinas*, ed. Richard A. Cohen (Albany, NY: SUNY, 1986), 25.
68. Charles Davis, *Soft Bodies in a Hard World: Spirituality for the Vulnerable* (Toronto: Anglican Book Centre, 1987), 15.
69. Ibid., 15.
70. Recall the closing words of the narrator Rieux in Camus' *The Plague*: "...the plague bacillus never dies or disappears for good; that it can lie dormant for years and years in furniture and linen-chests; that it bides its time in bedrooms, cellars, trunks, and bookshelves; and that perhaps the day would come when, for the bane and the enlightening of men, it would rouse up its rats again and send them forth to die in a happy city" (308).
71. Levinas, *Totality and Infinity*, 78.
72. Levinas and Kearney, "Dialogue," 32.
73. Taylor, *A Catholic Modernity?* 24.
74. Ibid., 35.
75. Charles Taylor, *Sources of the Self: The Making of the Modern Identity* (Cambridge, Mass.: Harvard University Press, 1989), 18.
76. Deleuze, "Nomad Thought," 144.
77. Gardiner, *The Dialogics of Critique*, 109.

Essay Five

A Critical Theory of Religious Insight

> When we criticize something, this is no arbitrary and impersonal event; it is…evidence of vital energies in us that are growing and shedding a skin. We negate and must negate because something in us wants to live and affirm—something that we perhaps do not know or see as yet.—This is said in favour of criticism.
>
> Friedrich Nietzsche, The Gay Science

A Prologue

WHAT IS the meaning and purpose of religious thought today?

Unlike past generations, confidence in the importance of this question is undoubtedly at a low ebb. While it may continue to be a pressing concern for theological discourse, its value for an expansive form of religio-philosophical reflection is less evident.[1] Yet as soon as this issue is framed as a question, a basic distance is achieved to reveal a certain "work of thought":[2] *In what way does the circumstantial fragility of contemporary religious thought release a new variety of religious thinking with its own, unique, critical moment and dynamic?*

Granted, even this more exact formulation of the matter may seem highly debatable. For what is religious thought *as such*? How can it be anything but "Jewish thought" or "Buddhist thought" or…? Beyond the aspiration to universal meaning that marked the study of religion during the 19th and 20th centuries, we now recognize that there is no honest way to evade the particularity of religious tradition and history.[3] In view of this consideration, we might more equitably describe our opening question as a *remnant* of a modern Christian thought struggling against its socio-cultural marginalization and intellectual deflation within a Western world turned secular. For to be preoccupied with the fate of "religious" meaning and purpose is to recollect the anxious moments of the modern Christian crisis of identity that was never quite resolved as it was normalized. As a result, a lack of self-assurance constantly shadows a battered Christian thought on the run.[4]

To cue the "post-Christian" situation in this way, however, is not to be wholly disparaging. For this novel predicament also encourages an important sense of modesty—theoretical and otherwise—that makes a distinct contribution to contemporary thought. Namely, the "post-Christian" situation as "post"; as a tradition splitting away from itself, not only yields a fragmented Christian context that marks the end of dogmatic certitude,[5] but augments a broader phenomenon in which unattached yet diverse religious contents—including Christian contents!—support reciprocal developments in critical *epistemology* and *ethics*. To explain—

As the substance of a destabilized religious deposit overflows its traditional cultural containers into ever wider forms of non-religious discourse, reticent *religious terms, themes, symbols*, and *ideas* resurface to "deterritorialize"[6] the established conceptual landscape. This religious substance become "nomadic"[7] serves to disrupt our prevailing (secular) ways of thinking, allowing us to see them as strange. This process of *dépaysement* works to illuminate the limits of thought as concealed by its conventionality. Once revealed, its congealed features melt away to disclose the possibility of pressing beyond the edges of what we have become in order to inscribe other boundaries of insight.[8] Thus, the unplanned circulation of a fractured religious heritage "problematizes"[9] the customary, while arousing a more critical conceptualization of what could be.[10]

However, more than a breakthrough in understanding is signalled by the transformative effect of the unchecked religious moment. For the critical detachment from ourselves also betrays the pressure of a fundamental "otherness" linked to a concern for the human being in need. Here the disturbing appeal for help from the "Other" occasions a cleft in the isolated "Self" that empties out as ethical response: that is, as a compassionate giving over to an exteriority that is *not us*. Far from natural, this *kenotic* outcome insinuates the upsurge of a religious content that intercedes in the form of a breach, throwing human Being into question. Thus an estranged religious substance inserts itself in relation to an ethics concerned to critically establish a way of *not* being in this world.

A question arises at this point: Is it not possible to gather and organize these fragments of religious thought and praxis so that their critico-ethical potential is made operative in relation to current forms of human existence? Indeed, is it not possible to articulate a new type of critical theory understood as "a critical theory of religious insight"?

In response to this query, the following essay begins with an examination of the early critical theory of Max Horkheimer (*"The Compassion of Critique"*); endeavours to mitigate its shortcomings with an assist from the moral reflections of Charles Taylor (*"The Best Account is Trumps"*); then presses on to champion the critical-theoretic facets of Emmanuel Levinas' philosophical ethics (*"God Concludes as Critique"*). To be sure, the argument is programmatic in character and raises numerous issues that cannot be addressed within the scope of its sweep. Nevertheless, the sweep itself is vital to outline if we to are to discern a *form of thought* whose reach includes religious terms, themes, symbols, and ideas become critical. That is, a form of thought in which religion helps to "separate out, from the contingency that has made us what we are, the possibility of no longer being, doing, or thinking, what we are do or think."[11]

The Compassion of Critique

There is something both exceptional and compelling about a form of critical thought driven by an *"Interesse an der Aufhebung des gesellschaftlichen Unrechts"*[12]—that is, by an "interest in the elimination of social injustice." Precisely what Max Horkheimer means by *"Interesse"* has never been adequately explained despite its apparent centrality.[13] While this ambiguity entails its own importance, it suffices to underscore that Horkheimer draws a fundamental link between the "consciously critical attitude"[14] on the one hand, and an abiding concern for the unnecessary suffering of human beings, on the other. Critical theory—or at least Horkheimer's version of it[15]—stems from a deeply felt response to "The wretchedness of our own time"[16] and a steadfast refusal to "compromise with continued misery."[17] Herein lies "the compassion of critique" as the effort to expose the true sources of useless suffering within the present age.

As Jürgen Habermas sees it, the compassion of critique represents the rear guard reaction of a "religiously tutored conscience"[18] spurned by an unyielding secular context. Taking up residence in the ruins of post-Christian thought,[19] Horkheimer, says Habermas, never abandons the discouraging intuition that "to seek to salvage an unconditional meaning without God is a futile undertaking." To be sure, there exists a definite tension in Horkheimer's work between the critical operations of thought and its share in a substantial notion of reason.[20] For Habermas, this incongruity betrays Horkheimer's failure to philosophically ground the normative orientation of critical theory. In a tenuous effort to span this lacunae, Horkheimer makes an unjustified appeal to a superseded "metaphysically grounded theology."²¹ Or as Horkheimer once expressed it:

> The appeal to an entirely other [*ein ganz Anderes*] than this world had primarily a socio-philosophical impetus. It led finally to a more positive evaluation of certain metaphysical trends, because the imperial "whole is untrue" (Adorno). The hope that earthly horror does not possess the last word is, to be sure, a non-scientific wish.²²

Undoubtedly, "The hope that earthly horror does not have the last word" is a constant for Horkheimer. However within his early essays, this hope has nothing to do with "a more positive evaluation of certain metaphysical trends." The initial expression of Horkheimer's critical theory is decidedly postmetaphysical. "When dialectic is freed of its connection with the exaggerated concept of isolated thought, self-determining and complete in itself, the theory defined by it necessarily loses the metaphysical character of final validity, the sanctity of a revelation, and becomes an element, itself transitory, intertwined in the fate of human beings."²³ Human knowledge, truth, and theory emerge from and are shaped by the ongoing historical reality of fallible human beings understood as social agents. The validity of their specific claims to truth or moral rightness cannot be formulated outside of the socio-historical conditions in which these claims occur. Both the value and vexation of the human enterprise stems from this always already limited context. "Every feature of the present age should be understood as a factor in a historical dynamic not as a manifestation of an eternal being."²⁴

It is precisely this postmetaphysical approach that confirms the critical recognition of unnecessary human suffering. Says Horkheimer, "solidarity with struggling, suffering human beings obviously tends to make one apathetic toward metaphysical assurances."²⁵ It does so because the pain of human suffering cuts right through those metaphysical modes of thought that dismiss the pathology of suffering as a logical consequence of past wrongs, a this-worldly premium for other-worldly bliss, or simply as natural and inevitable. The metaphysical attachment to eternal being is exposed for what it truly is: a devotion to a particular form of life that maintains itself at the expense of others.

The compassion of critique can be said to still Habermas's protest. For solidarity with the weak and the humiliated does not call for a "metaphysically grounded theology" as it does its critique. Yet to blunt Habermas's point here does not protect Horkheimer from its sting: the failure to philosophically ground the normative orientation of critical theory. Horkheimer's "appeal to an entirely other than this world" may disclose a paucity of philosophical thought on this issue. Unable to clarify the content of a critical reason on side with the vanquished, Horkheimer hints at a veiled notion of God that enjoins a fairly enigmatic vindication. On the other hand, this gesture may equally serve to disrupt the very notion of an immanent or systematic "philosophical grounding" altogether. *This is to say, that "The appeal to an entirely other than this world" may signal a non-philosophical exteriority whose very outsideness is able to install both the critical distance and moral weight vital to the compassion of critique.* This possibility need not betray a theological obfuscation as Habermas suggests. Rather, it may reveal a conceptual exit toward new critical boundaries established by recasting *religious terms*, *themes*, *symbols*, and *ideas* in relation to the "interest in the elimination of social injustice."

The pathway toward realizing this new configuration of thought is glimpsed in Horkheimer's 1933 essay, "Materialism and Morality." Here he endeavours to explain the materialist critique of Bourgeois morality. The goal: to expose the ideological function of this morality while simultaneously illuminating its significance for the potential form and content of humane experience.

Horkheimer begins: "Materialism sees in morality an expression of life of determinate individuals and seeks to understand it in terms of the conditions of its emergence and passing, not for the sake of truth in itself but rather in connection with determinate historical forces."[26] Morality is a decidedly finite affair, shaped by extant socio-cultural realities. Its analysis is significant for what it reveals about the meaning of the current historical situation rather than the disclosure of some timeless truth. A critical-materialist approach to morality "presumes no transhistorical authority behind morality;"[27] contends that "There is no eternal realm of values;"[28] and argues that "Binding moral laws do not exist."[29] It rejects the entire notion of a metaphysically grounded morality.[30]

In the case of Bourgeois morality, the struggle to achieve economic advantage over others is advanced as the most important facet of human life. Such an ethic becomes "the natural law under which individual life proceeds."[31] Historically conditioned values, then, are frozen in time as if they were absolute and unalterable. An economic practice that demands victimization in order to properly function thus appears "natural." The task of a postmetaphysical critique is to reveal the conditional base of such a "naturalism" so as to illuminate its role within the perpetuation of social injustice. Critique thus fixes itself along side forces intent upon social change:[32] it endeavours to become "the theoretical aspect of efforts to abolish existing misery [*die theoretische Seite der Anstrengungen, das vorhandene Elend abzuschaffen*]."[33]

Yet it is for this same reason that Horkheimer cannot simply dismiss the whole of morality as mere ideology or false consciousness.[34] For the "theoretical aspect of efforts to abolish existing misery" entails a moral moment that cannot be accounted for by a theory concerned to overcome morality as a Bourgeois social phenomena. It is in response to this dilemma that Horkheimer's version of critical theory evokes an alternative sense of morality that hinges on a religious sensibility in need of further thought. Horkheimer avers to a point of resistance within Kantian moral philosophy which, he believes, motions toward a characterization of the "moral sentiment" that significantly diverges from the reigning Bourgeois social ethic. Horkheimer writes:

> Moral sentiment has something to do with love, for "love, reverence, yearning for perfection, longing, all these things are inherent in an end" [Nietzsche]. However, this love has nothing to do with the person as economic subject or an item in the property of the one who loves, but rather as a potential member of a happy humanity. It is not directed at the role and standing of a particular individual in civil life, but at his neediness and powers, which point toward the future. Unless the aim of a future happy life for all, which admittedly arises not on the basis of a revelation but out of the privation of the present, is included in the description of this love, it proves impossible to define. To all, inasmuch as they are, after all, human beings, it wishes the free development of their creative powers. To love it appears as if all living beings have a claim to happiness, for which it would not in the least ask for any justification or grounds.[35]

In this passage, Horkheimer is cautiously circling about the prospect of transcending the modern emphasis on possessive individualism and instrumental thought. It is a question of moving beyond the cognizance of other human beings as mere objects of control or pleasure.[36] Yet the basic drift of Horkheimer's overall argument indicates that this is an extremely powerful inclination that is not easily expropriated.[37] Its overcoming demands a *unique interruption* that can disturb the habituation to power and struggle as normal. Thus the notion and ideal of "love" is evoked. The very feel of Horkheimer's presentation intimates that this is no ordinary love. Something extraordinary is straining to pierce its humanitarian cast: *"un étrange amour"*—to borrow an apt phrase from Albert Camus[38]—that furthers a self-emptying, kenotic love capable of granting primacy to the needs of the other human being over those of the Self. This pre-eminence seems to implore the gift of an unrestricted love that as gratuitous is radically other than self-serving expediency. "It is the *kenosis* put into practice by Christ as man: the act of emptying out every element of individual autonomy and self-sufficiency, and realizing the life of love and communion."[39] Or in the words of Emmanuel Levinas, it is "that which ensures being, elevation and holiness in the *other than myself*..."[40] *Of course this is not the main thrust of Horkheimer's message.*[41] Yet if morality is to be more than an "optional extra"[42] for critical theory, then the tacit connotations of Horkheimer's view beckon creative enhancement. Only in some such manner could the trace of a love that "has nothing to do with the person as economic subject or an item in the property of the one who loves, but rather as a potential member of a happy humanity," be recalled, sustained, developed and furthered.

Toward that end, it would seem to logically follow that the moral sentiment serve to ground the normative orientation of Horkheimer's critical theory understood as "the compassion of critique." Yet it is just this logic that Horkheimer renounces. Love, happiness, compassion, etc., do not "in the least ask for any justification or grounds."[43] They do not because such sentiments represent immediate human responses to injustice which, as spontaneous, constitute genuine expressions of protest against the powers that be. To demand their theoretical justification as necessary for the recognition of their validity is to deflect the critical force of these sentiments until their rationalization is complete—which can never be fully achieved.[44] Thus, "Logic...remains silent and grants no pre-eminence to moral conviction."[45]

Yet this justificatory deficit[46] exposes a curious discrepancy in Horkheimer's position in which any theoretical verification of morality is identified with a metaphysical claim to unconditional meaning.[47] A postmetaphysical exploration of morality must therefore reject its theoretical embodiment as essential to its critical contribution to contemporary thought. However, given Horkheimer's presentation of the moral sentiment in relation to the compassion of critique, such a division of explanatory power is extremely awkward. For one, it frustrates the critical ideal that there can be "no areas set aside to which thought is not to be applied."[48] For another, it suggests a troubling moral positivism which intends to cut through the risk of objectification by excluding rational analysis altogether. In each case, the larger critical goal is negated since reflection is required of all involved experience and thought whose meaning can be reasonably doubted. This surely holds true for the moral sentiment: "...morality itself is problematical, not merely in its content, but in its supposed existence as a dimension of practical thought or social evaluation at all."[49] It is hardly immoderate to demand some form of rational justification.

But which form? And for which content?

It is best to advance a postmetaphysical form of moral thought and expression that can evade the antipodal consequences of Horkheimer's position by recognizing moral ideas, themes, and terms as necessary for any theoretical locution. It is also worthwhile to explore the ways in which this formation releases the religious fragments for additional work. With these issues in mind we now consider the contribution of Charles Taylor.

The Best Account is Trumps

"What makes the human life worth living?" So begins Charles Taylor's expansive enquiry into morality.[50] Aside from pondering issues like human dignity, respect, or autonomy, etc., morality, notes Taylor, involves complex philosophical and spiritual frameworks that not only determine what it is right to do, but shape what it is good to be. This is a far more penetrating operation. To make one's way here with any degree of profundity, a moral response of sufficient depth is required, one that involves "strong evaluation."[51] This comprises the use of contrastive, discriminatory terms like "good or bad," "better or worse," "higher or lower," "authentic or inauthentic" etc., which serve to discern the form and content of the moral life. The full gravity of these terms only emerge once we recognize that they constitute independent standards by which the value of our moral achievement is assessed.[52] Strong evaluation motions toward the objectivity and truth of our moral sentiments. They help to determine what is or should be of the utmost importance for living out our lives in a worthy fashion. Strong evaluation is not an optional extra either.

However, it could become just that unless we learn to develop our powers of "articulation." In the broadest possible terms, "articulation," for Taylor, delineates the effort to express and cultivate a moral vision of things; a "thought-full" thematization of what we consider to be "the good life." More narrowly, these articulations constitute "ontological accounts"[53] of human being lived morally. They are "ontological" because they deal with what we consider to be most real about our moral existence; marking those features which, after intelligent examination and practical corroboration, tend to hold. Actually, these ontological constructs furnish our very mode of access to the moral domain. "We find the sense of life through articulating it. ...Finding a sense to life depends on framing meaningful expressions which are adequate."[54] As we reach through to this level of articulacy, we are drawn ever closer to the various sources that empower our moral lives.[55] That is why words can be so influential and forceful: they both form and transform moral identities.[56] It is also why some terms, symbols, or narratives are deemed more important than others: some prove to be inescapable for articulating an adequate moral framework. To abandon such forms of expression because they fail to measure up to some rationalistic standard or appear to be too "poetic" or "spiritual" etc., is to relinquish access to the root inspirations of the ample moral life. Without them, we become morally impoverished.

This is not to suggest that complete articulacy is possible. As Taylor contends, "articulation can by its very nature never be completed. We clarify one language with another, which in turn can be further unpacked, and so on."[57] Our ontological account concerning what makes life worth living constitutes an ongoing process of change and revision. Thus articulation demands argumentation whereby moral development and growth is possible. What does this involve?

Taylor is eager to ground a viable alternative to moral ontologies rooted in modern rationalistic models of argument and proof. Here moral phenomena are considered to be "true" insofar that they obtain a kind of objectivity that transcends all historical and cultural supposition that stem from the particularity of human existence. In this way, all rational persons who encounter "real" moral phenomena ought to be able to concede its universal validity upon due rational demonstration.[58] At its extreme point, this implies that moral argument should be able to convince others of the absolute "truth" of our position even when they share nothing of our moral perspective.[59] However, this measure of moral matters cannot be satisfied, and part of the postmetaphysical philosophical task is to realize that we shouldn't even try. To do so, contends Taylor, is to change the subject since "Moral argumentation and explanation go on only within a world shaped by our deepest moral responses...No argument can take someone from a neutral stance...to insight into moral ontology."[60]

This does not mean, however, that our ontological accounts are mere fictions. This suspicion is dispelled once we recognize the indispensable role of articulation. For what better measure of things do we have, asks Taylor, than those crucial terms, ideas, and narratives which—after critical reflection and suitable correction—appear to make the best sense out of our moral lives? After all, it is precisely such communicative features of the human life that grant access to the moral domain as moral. This holds true, moreover, for even the most value-laden, culturally-specific, historically-determined sources that may inform our moral orientation. To deny them explanatory power simply because they fail to conform to some modern notion of universality is to advance moral inarticulacy as the norm.[61] Thus, we must recognize how problematic it is to bar the terms that shape our moral lives from contributing to the development of moral argument and theory.[62] When we do allow them full entry, then our ontological accounts must be argued and presented as a "best account" of the moral life that we are able to articulate at the moment. In Taylor's words:

> What we need to *explain* is people living their lives; the terms in which they cannot avoid living them cannot be removed from the explanandum, unless we can propose other terms in which they could live them more clairvoyantly. We cannot just leap outside of these terms altogether, on the grounds that their logic doesn't fit some model of "science" and that we know a priori that human beings must be explicable in this "science." ...The terms we select have to make sense across the whole range of both explanatory and life uses. The terms indispensable for the latter are part of the story that makes best sense of us, unless and until we can replace them with more clairvoyant substitutes. The result of this search for clairvoyance yields the best account we can give at any given time, and no epistemological or metaphysical considerations of a more general kind about science or nature can justify setting this aside. The best account...is trumps.[63]

Backtracking to Horkheimer's version of critical theory, we can now suggest that "love," "compassion," "solidarity," and "happiness" represent the vital moral terms through which the socially engaged agent gains access to the very "interest in the elimination of social injustice." *Without these types of expression, no such interest; and without this interest, no critical theory.* It is most unlikely that this integral alliance can either be sustained or deepened by secretly drawing upon a moral form of life while shrinking from its larger justification as Horkheimer does. To deny morality any conceptual purchase within the larger "explanandum" cannot but undermine the future of critical theory.[64] To surpass this dilemma is to adopt a different view: "The terms we select have to make sense across the whole range of both explanatory and life uses. The terms indispensable for the latter are part of the story that makes best sense of us..."

The compassion of critique is rooted in "an ontological account" or moral vision whose terms, sensibilities, and goals are indispensable for critical theory as critical. To dismiss or obscure this moral vision is to sabotage the theory altogether. To cultivate or enrich its moral form, however, presents its own kind of concerns. For instance, to validate the morally pertinent underscores the culturally-specific and historically-determined character of its "strong evaluation." To further unfold this trait is to grapple with the distinctive sources of religious insight at work within the compassion of critique. To advance this particular association as key is to postulate that some terms, narratives, and symbols are more important than others. Thus, language shifts, mutates, and alters. Yet to suggest this is already to insinuate a set of clairvoyant substitutes. And "The result of this search for clairvoyance yields the best account we can give at any given time…" With this proviso in hand, we move on to examine Emmanuel Levinas.

God Concludes As Critique

Approaching the Jewish philosophy of Emmanuel Levinas from the outside may be well worthwhile. To come at his thought from within, may be more inhibiting. Pressing beyond the internal pressure to mirror the philosopher's uniqueness is vital if one intends to build. While all such construction demands a selective use of materials that knowingly abandons the whole, anxiety over this surrender cannot be our concern. Ours rather involves the clarification of one language or set of terms by another. *Thus, a radical shift in tone and feeling asserts itself in order to make the point.* Recall Horkheimer's basic moral intuition: the encounter with the other human being in need as the beginning of a critique rooted in the longing for social justice. Yet this longing also echoes a religious moment that makes itself felt as a strange form of kenotic love preoccupied with the concerns of the other human being over those of the Self. While Horkheimer dilutes this moment in a variety of ways, our best effort to redeem this intertwining of themes claims clairvoyant substitutes from an ethical understanding of God that concludes as critique.

To begin: the other human being is not merely "other [*l'Autre*]" with a difference purely relative to me as the "same [*le Même*]." For the other to be truly other-than-me, there must be a real distance or distinction to ensure the difference. The otherness of the "Other [*l'Auturi*)" resides in an exteriority that cannot be neutralized by reducing the Other to another "me."[65] Such a level of control cannot be had without doing violence to the Other. Granted, this is a real temptation. The Other can seem extremely threatening as the stranger who trespasses against the freedom of the self-enclosed subject.[66] Thus the impulse to lash out against the Other as a way to protect the Self. At the same time (and precisely at the same time), the intrusion of the Other provokes an ethical charge that cannot be wholly absolved. The difference between the two moments is not insignificant.

The original inspiration for the ethical upsurge is, according to Levinas, "the epiphany of the face as a face."[67] By "face," Levinas does not mean the actual visage with its range of expressions, but a mode of existing that speaks, calls out (*ekklesia*?), pleads for help and understanding.[68] Here the face is highly vulnerable and exposed. The face implores: "Do not take advantage of my vulnerability! Do not use my weakness against me! Do not injure, harm, or kill me!" Of course, human beings not only consistently ignore these appeals but seize the moment to advance themselves against the Other in both subtle and brutal ways. In contrast, the ethical response grants primacy to the concerns of the Other over those of the Self. The Other comes first. The ethical being greets the face—bare, unprotected, and desperate for fellowship—as an event that uproots the subject from the Self, shattering the drive for survival, throwing one's existence and power into question.[69] Humanity's facility for cruelty is here averted under pressure from something "otherwise-than-being [*autrement qu'être*]."[70] Or, ethics emerges from "a relation without relation": a relation where the bond does not overwhelm the separation, and where the separation does not destroy the bond.[71] *It is a relation—with something we are not.* Thus the idea of God comes to mind.[72]

Following Levinas, God is first and foremost an ethical God: interested in the plight of humankind and the moral character of their interactions. Thus "The ethical call to conscience...remains an essentially religious vocation."[73] Yet it is only by attending to the needs of the other human being that one encounters the divine at all.[74] "There can be no 'knowledge' [*connaissance*] of God," writes the author, "separated from the relationship with men."[75] For this reason Levinas contends that "God rises to his supreme and ultimate presence as correlative to the justice rendered unto men."[76] Or could we say, the welcoming of God in humanity as critical social theory?

This religio-ethical vision of things hinges on a negative though crucial dynamic: "It involves a calling into question of oneself, a critical attitude which is itself produced in the face of the other [*L'Autre*] and under his authority."[77] As Levinas sees it, without this attitude there can be no justice. Justice is inspired by seriously doubting and inspecting any assumed possession of the world.[78] On the other side of this assumption lies the promise of true fellowship. However, this expectation is but a consequence of an ethical encounter—"produced in the face of the other and under his authority"—that bears witness to God's proximity. It is only with *His* breach in Being that the Other can be perceived and approached as Other. It is only with *His* breach in Being that one's existence can be limited or curbed in view of the Other. It is only with *His* breach in Being that one can give themselves away to the other human being in need. That is why, again, "God rises to his supreme and ultimate presence as correlative to the justice rendered unto men."[79] And it is also why the critical attitude is key to this entire religio-ethical analysis. Says Levinas, "transcendence, the welcoming of the other [*l'Autre*] by the same [*le Même*], of the Other [*l'Auturi*] by me, is concretely produced as the calling into question of the same by the other [*l'Autre*], that is, as the ethics that accomplishes the critical essence of knowledge [*l'éthique qui accomplit l'essence critique du savoir*]."[80]

Doesn't this "critical essence of knowledge" constitute the kind of "knowledge which brings its own obligations with it" as Horkheimer once described critical theory?[81] Are we not, then, on the cusp of "a critical theory of religious insight"?

Much of Levinas' work appears to be hostile to theory, thematization, and representation as that which reduces the Other to the same by making it "comprehensible."[82] Yet on closer inspection, he advances an alternative understanding of theory *as such*; one that aligns itself with the very breach in Being that establishes the ethical relation. Levinas suggests that the exteriority that is evoked by the Other is closely tied to the exteriority vital to theoretical analysis.[83] As he sees it, both forms of detachment are necessary to settle the truth of things.[84] Still, there would seem to be two different types of detachment, and with that, two types of theory: the ontological and the critical.

As ontological, theory aspires to explain the Other by reducing her or him to Being or to thought emerging from the knowing-subject. "The relation with Being that is enacted as ontology consists in neutralizing the existent in order to comprehend or grasp it. It is hence not a relation with the other [*l'autre*] as such but the reduction of the other to the same [*l'Autre au Même*]."[85] As a result, exteriority and alterity are absorbed by a comprehension without remainder.[86] Theory as ontology is an exercise in freedom that refuses to be thrown into question. "Such is the definition of freedom: to maintain oneself against the other [*l'autre*], despite every relation with the other [*l'autre*]…"[87] Ontology negates the obligations that stem from the Other. God is eclipsed, and the inhumane moment is given free reign. Levinas concludes that ontological theory is a theory of power and injustice.

Against this, Levinas advances an alternative form of theory that arises from the religio-ethical rupture in Being that calls into question the ways of the same. The awakening of responsibility that comes to be via the encounter with the Other and with God, partially resolves itself in the exercise of critique—a critique of the ontological freedoms that do violence to the Other. "The essence of reason consists not in securing for man a foundation and powers, but in calling him into question and inviting him to justice [*à le mettre en question et à l'inviter à la justice*]."[88] It is an exercise that therefore points toward another form of freedom—a critical freedom—that seeks to interrupt humanity's inhumanity in the name of justice. Or, through this ethico-critical relation to the Other, God is drawn out, made manifest, "disincarnated [*désincarné*]," revealed.[89] So the divine invests itself in "theoretical efforts to abolish existing misery."[90]

A Postscript

What is the meaning and purpose of religious thought today?

If critical theory constitutes a refusal to compromise with existing misery in this world, then a critical theory of religious insight endeavours to illumine the religious fragments adrift within that refusal. To cultivate these moments as a project first asks for an important shift in perspective. It requires an approach that considers the terms of one's discourse as "more-or-less" adequate until critically informed substitutes are suggested as clearer, more substantial, more intelligent: "the best account is trumps." No appeal to "reason" or "science" or "utility" or to any other culturally specific category pretending to be absolute can automatically negate the contribution of another language, perspective, or discipline if indeed it adds to a better account of things. And this "better" can only be fully assessed in relation to the use of a particular type of language; in relation to the ebb and flow of the discourse itself; and in relation to problems (temporarily) solved and the emerging sense of added insight.[91] Taylor's proposal suggests that this is as good as it gets for all truly moral, philosophical, religious discourses, and, we must add, critical-theoretic discourses.

In line with this proposal, Levinas' religio-ethical philosophy has been brought to bear upon the shape and content of critical theory. Clear from this encounter is the idea of God as central to Levinas' critique. This idea, and its associated themes and terms, cannot be dismissed from that critique without fundamentally altering or even destroying it as such. *For the uniqueness and the value of Levinas' critique depends upon an understanding of God as the ethical force that can interrupt, subvert, or throw into question the self-centred existence that creates and spreads human suffering in this world. The ethical God is also a critical God who, as "otherwise than being," problematizes the ways of the world by interjecting an "other-worldly" moment that averts the human propensity for cruelty.* At the level of theory, such divinely inspired problematization shows up as a critique of unimpeded freedom; as a critique of those forms of thought and action that reduce the Other to the same for the purposes of control. On the other side of this critique lies the promise and prospect of justice for all. And it is in this promise and prospect that God reigns supreme.

It is evident that the Jewish and Christian view of God as an ethical force is pivotal. While the ethical take on these religious traditions hardly exhausts their full meaning; and while these same two traditions cannot be said to lock in the scope of a critical theory of religious insight, both Judaism and Christianity remain key given the historical, cultural, and social context that animates this analysis. Yet much still needs to be said about Levinas' Jewish thought and its Christian appropriation. As an observation, Christian thinkers often assimilate a Jewish idea, term, narrative, or concern as if such content were always already available for Christian use in virtue of being the historical "feeder" for the Christian faith. By contrast, relatively few Jewish thinkers are inspired to deal with Christian themes in virtue of the Jewish character of Jesus or *The New Testament*. Does the ease of the Christian appropriation constitute a subtle form of post-Christian triumphalism? Well in some cases it does. However, remembering the fragmentation of religion and the open circulation of religious ideas, the dilemma as I have just framed it is less pressing. Nonetheless, the Christian appropriation of Jewish thought cannot but have integral consequences for the nature and character of the post-Christian self-understanding and representation. In the case of the Christian engagement of Levinas, much critical work still needs to be done.[92]

Whatever the outcome of this endeavour, it remains evident that the development of a critical theory of religious insight unfolds neither as an accident nor as an arbitrary construct but as an inherent moment within the formation of critical theory itself. This holds true for the critical theory hammered out by Horkheimer whose "interest in the elimination of social injustice" evokes a moral moment with distinct religious undertones. While this characteristic hints at the plausibility of a non-philosophical inspiration for critical theory, Horkheimer backs away, refusing to give the religio-ethical facet of his work any explanatory power. Here, the critical interest languishes. To revitalize it is to build upon a missed opportunity, steering critical theory toward the religio-ethical concern for the Other as the best way to establish the compassion of critique.

This possibility doesn't claim to exhaust the meaning and form of critical theory. Nor does it claim that critical theory is always already religious or theological, as some have wrongly argued.[93] Nor does it even suggest that herein lies the ultimate form of contemporary religious thought. What it does claim is an untried form of critical theory whose religio-ethical cast and content contributes to the venture of contemporary thought by working through the fragility of religious thought today.

Notes

1. I am thinking here of various "existential" thinkers such as Martin Buber, Gabriel Marcel, Karl Jaspers, Nicola Berdyev etc., who deal with substantive religious themes while pointing beyond the particularity of the content to affirm insights deemed vital for those beyond the circle and community of faith. For a contemporary instance of this approach, see Ludwig Heyde, *The Weight of Finitude: On the Philosophical Question of God*, trans. Alexander Harmsen and William Desmond (Albany, NY: SUNY, 1999).
2. Michel Foucault, "Polemics, Politics, and Problematizations," trans. Robert Hurley and others, in *Ethics: Subjectivity and Truth*, vol. 1 of *The Essential Works of Foucault, 1954–1984*, ed. Paul Rabinow (New York: The New Press, 1997), 118.
3. Walter H. Capps, *Religious Studies: The Making of a Discipline* (Minneapolis: Fortress Press, 1995), 1–104.
4. Jürgen Habermas, "Transcendence From Within, Transcendence in This World," in *Habermas, Modernity, and Public Theology*, eds. Don S. Browning and Francis Schüssler Fiorenza (New York: Crossroad, 1992).
5. Charles Davis, *Temptations of Religion* (New York: Harper and Row, 1973), 1–27.
6. Gilles Deleuze, "Nomad Thought," in *The New Nietzsche*, ed. David B. Allison (Cambridge, Mass.: MIT Press, 1985), 144.
7. Ibid., 148.
8. Michel Foucault, "What is Enlightenment?" trans. Robert Hurley and others, in *Ethics: Subjectivity and Truth*, vol. 1 of *The Essential Works of Foucault, 1954–1984*, ed. Paul Rabinow (New York: The New Press, 1997), 315.
9. Foucault, "Polemics, Politics, and Problematizations."
10. Craig Calhoun, *Critical Social Theory: Culture, History, and the Challenge of Difference* (Oxford: Blackwell, 1995), xviii, 9.
11. Foucault, "What is Enlightenment?" 315–316.
12. Max Horkheimer, "Materialismus und Moral," in *Kritische Theorie*, Band II (Frankfurt am Main: Fischer Verlag, 1968), 190.
13. See Jürgen Habermas, *Knowledge and Human Interest*, trans. Jeremy Shapiro (Boston:

Beacon Press, 1971); Michael Peillon, *The Concept of Interest in Social Theory* (Lewiston, NY: Edwin Mellon Press, 1990); Herbert Schnädelbach, "Max Horkheimer and the Philosophy of German Idealism," in *On Max Horkheimer: New Perspectives*, eds. Selya Benhabib, Wolfgang Boneß, and John McCole (Cambridge, Mass.: MIT Press, 1993), 295–302.

14. Max Horkheimer, "Traditional and Critical Theory," in *Critical Theory: Selected Essays*, trans. Matthew J. O'Connell and others (New York: Continuum Press, 1972), 229.
15. See Douglas Kellner, *Critical Theory, Marxism, and Modernity* (Baltimore: Johns Hopkins University Press, 1989), 15, 30–33, 237; and Rolf Wiggershaus, *The Frankfurt School: Its History, Theories, and Political Significance*, trans. Michael Robertson (Cambridge, Mass.: MIT Press, 1995), 6, 48–50.
16. Max Horkheimer, "Materialism and Metaphysics," in *Critical Theory: Selected Essays*, trans. Matthew J. O'Connell and others (New York: Continuum Press, 1972), 24.
17. Max Horkheimer, "Postscript," in *Critical Theory: Selected Essays*, trans. Matthew J. O'Connell and others (New York: Continuum Press, 1972), 248.
18. Jürgen Habermas, "To Seek to Salvage an Unconditional Meaning Without God is a Futile Undertaking: Reflections on a Remark of Max Horkheimer," in *Justification and Application: Remarks on Discourse Ethics*, trans. Ciaran P. Cronin (Cambridge, Mass.: MIT Press, 1993), 134.
19. Or is it post-Jewish thought? The degree to which Horkheimer's perspective (as well as the other members of the Frankfurt School) was either influenced by or representative of a modern Jewish thinking is ambivalent. While both Wiggerhaus (in *The Frankfurt School*, 4–5) and Calhoun (in *Critical Social Theory*, 17) suggest a relatively important correlation between the Jewish background of the Frankfurt School and its theoretical production, Martin Jay seems to dismiss it in his pioneering study, *The Dialectical Imagination: A History of the Frankfurt School and the Institute of Social Research, 1923–1950* (Berkeley: University of California Press, 1973), 33. For my part, it seems clear that Horkheimer tends to evoke Christian themes, if he evokes anything at all. Consider, for example, the resonance between his characterization of the "critical theorist" and "Jesus Christ." As he puts it in "Traditional and Critical Theory": "...the theoretician is also at times an enemy and criminal, at times a solitary utopian; even after his death the question of what he really was is not decided. The historical significance of his work is not self-evident; it rather depends on men speaking and acting in such a way as to justify it" (220).
20. Jay, *The Dialectical Imagination*, 53, 63.
21. Habermas, "To Seek To Salvage an Unconditional Meaning Without God," 135.
22. Max Horkheimer, "Forward," in Martin Jay, *The Dialectical Imagination: A History of the Frankfurt School and the Institute of Social Research, 1923–1950* (Berkeley: University of California Press, 1973), xxvi.
23. Max Horkheimer, "On the Problem of Truth," in *Between Philosophy and the Social Sciences: Selected Early Writings*, trans. G. Frederick Hunter, Matthew S. Kramer, and John Torpey (Cambridge, Mass.: MIT Press, 1993), 191.
24. Max Horkheimer, "Remarks on Philosophical Anthropology," in *Between Philosophy and the Social Sciences: Selected Early Writings*, trans. G. Frederick Hunter, Matthew S.

Kramer, and John Torpey (Cambridge, Mass.: MIT Press, 1993), 161.
25. Ibid., 160.
26. Max Horkheimer, "Materialism and Morality," in *Between Philosophy and the Social Sciences: Selected Early Writings*, trans. G. Frederick Hunter, Matthew S. Kramer, and John Torpey (Cambridge, Mass.: MIT Press, 1993), 32.
27. Ibid., 32.
28. Ibid., 33.
29. Ibid.
30. Horkheimer, "Materialism and Metaphysics," 44.
31. Horkheimer, "Materialism and Morality," 19.
32. Horkheimer, "Traditional and Critical Theory," 215.
33. Horkheimer, "Materialism and Morality," 32.
34. Ibid., 22.
35. Ibid., 34–35.
36. On this issue Horkheimer writes: "Kant describes marriage as the 'joining together of two people of the opposite sex for the lifelong mutual ownership of their sexual attributes' and speaks of the 'equality of possessions' of the married couple not merely in terms of material goods, but also in terms of 'two people who mutually own each other.'" Much the same is said of Freud who, according to Horkheimer, argues that "the loved person appears mainly as the means to fulfil [eroto-genic zone] stimulation. On this point, one is struck by the way in which Freud's theory is an elaboration of Kant's definition of marriage" ("Materialism and Morality," 34).
37. As Horkheimer notes in the same essay: "In an epoch in which the domination of the possessive instincts is the natural law of humanity, and in which by Kant's definition each individual sees the other above all as a means to his own ends, morality represents the concern for the development and happiness of life as a whole. *Even the opponents of traditional morality presuppose in their critique an indeterminate moral sentiment with such strivings*" ("Materialism and Morality," 30. Italics added).
38. Albert Camus, *L'Homme Révolté* (Paris: Gallimard, 1951), 364.
39. Christos Yannaras, *The Freedom of Morality*, trans. Elizabeth Briere (Crestwood, NY: St. Vladimir's Seminary Press, 1984), 52–53.
40. Emmanuel Levinas, "Judaism and Kenosis," in *The Time of the Nations*, trans. Michael B. Smith (Bloomington: Indiana University Press), 125.
41. Nevertheless, revisit note 19.
42. Charles Taylor, *Sources of the Self: The Making of the Modern Identity* (Cambridge, Mass.: Harvard University Press, 1989), 41.
43. Horkheimer, "Materialism and Morality," 35.
44. Schnädelbach, "Horkheimer and the Philosophy of German Idealism," 292.
45. Horkheimer, "Materialism and Morality," 33.
46. Schnädelbach, "Horkheimer and the Philosophy of German Idealism," 300.
47. Horkheimer, "Materialism and Metaphysics," 23.
48. Ibid., 39.
49. Bernard Williams, *Moral Luck* (Cambridge: Cambridge University Press, 1981), x.

50. The interpretation of Taylor's work is growing all the time. See, for example, Ruth Abbey, *Charles Taylor* (Princeton: Princeton University Press, 2000); Bernard Gagnon, *La Philosophie Morale et Politique de Charles Taylor* (Québec: Les Presses de l'Université Laval, 2002); Janie Pélaby, *Charles Taylor: Penseur de la Pluralité* (Ste. Foy: Presses de l'Université de Laval, 2001); and Nicholas H. Smith, *Charles Taylor: Meaning, Morals, and Modernity* (Cambridge: Polity Press, 2002).
51. Taylor, *Sources of the Self*, 4. Also see Charles Taylor, "What is Human Agency?" in *Human Agency and Language* (Cambridge: Cambridge University Press, 1985), 15–44.
52. Taylor, *Sources of the Self*, 42.
53. Ibid., 8.
54. Ibid., 18.
55. Ibid., 92.
56. Ibid., 96.
57. Ibid., 34.
58. This, of course, is Jürgen Habermas's position as outlined within his theory of communicative action and discourse ethics. For Taylor's critique of Habermas see his essay, "Language and Society," trans. Jeremy Gaines and Doris L. Jones, in *Communicative Action: Essays on Jürgen Habermas' Theory of Communicative Action*, eds. Axel Honneth and Hans Joas (Cambridge, Mass.: MIT Press, 1991), 23–35.
59. Taylor, *Sources of the Self*, 71–72.
60. Ibid., 8.
61. Ibid., 57.
62. Ibid., 58.
63. Ibid.
64. It is for perhaps this reason that the critical theory of the Frankfurt School tends to develop into a philosophy of despair. On this issue see Jürgen Habermas' essay, "The Entwinement of Myth and Enlightenment: Max Horkheimer and Theodor Adorno," in *The Philosophical Discourse of Modernity: Twelve Lectures*, trans. Frederick G. Lawrence (Cambridge, Mass.: MIT Press, 1987), 106–130.
65. Emmanuel Levinas, *Totality and Infinity: An Essay on Exteriority*, trans. Alphonso Lingis (Pittsburgh: Duquesne Press, 1969), 38–39.
66. Ibid., 181.
67. Ibid., 75.
68. Ibid., 199.
69. Ibid., 43.
70. See Emmanuel Levinas, *Otherwise than Being: Or, Beyond Essence*, trans. Alphonso Lingis (The Hague: Matinus Nijhoff, 1981).
71. Levinas, *Totality and Infinity*, 80.
72. Richard Kearney and Emmanuel Levinas, "Dialogue with Emmanuel Levinas," in *Face to Face with Levinas*, ed. Richard A. Cohen (Albany, NY: SUNY, 1986), 25.
73. Ibid.
74. Levinas, *Totality and Infinity*, 79.
75. Ibid., 78.

76. Ibid.
77. Ibid., 81.
78. Ibid., 75–76.
79. Ibid., 78.
80. Ibid., 43.
81. Horkheimer, "Traditional and Critical Theory," 241.
82. Thus Levinas' philosophy is examined in a work on "anti-theory." See Dwight Furrow, *Against Theory: Continental and Analytic Challenges in Moral Philosophy* (New York: Routledge, 1995), 139–160.
83. Levinas, *Totality and Infinity*, 81.
84. Ibid., 61. Also see Edith Wyschogrod, *Emmanuel Levinas: The Problem of Ethical Metaphysics* (The Hague: Martinus Nijhoff, 1974), 91.
85. Levinas, *Totality and Infinity*, 45–46.
86. Ibid., 123–124.
87. Ibid., 46.
88. Ibid., 88.
89. Ibid., 79.
90. Horkheimer, "Materialism and Morality," 32.
91. Charles Taylor, *Philosophical Arguments* (Cambridge, Mass.: Harvard University Press, 1995), 34–60.
92. Important contributions toward this end include Roger Burggraeve, *From Self-Development to Solidarity: An Ethical Reading of Human Desire in its Socio-Political Relevance According to Levinas* (Leuven: Peters, 1985); Jean-Luc Marion, *God Without Being*, trans. Thomas A. Carlson (Chicago: University of Chicago Press, 1991); and Lucien Richard, "The Possibility of the Incarnation According to Emmanuel Levinas," *Studies in Religion/Sciences Religieuses* 17 (1988): 391–405.
93. This is the basic "argumentative" approach of numerous "critical" theologians. See for example Charles Davis, *Theology and Political Society* (Cambridge: Cambridge University Press, 1980); J.B. Metz, *Faith in History and Society: Toward a Practical Fundamental Theology*, trans. David Smith (New York: Crossroad, 1980); Helmult Peukert, *Science, Action, and Fundamental Theology: Toward a Theology of Communicative Action*, trans. James Bohman (Cambridge, Mass.: MIT Press, 1986). For a critique of the latter see Marc P. Lalonde, *Critical Theology and the Challenge of Jürgen Habermas: Toward a Critical Theory of Religious Insight* (New York: Peter Lang, 1999), 43–61.

Conclusion

THERE IS an outstanding issue that I would like to address here, one evoked by the very title of the project. Namely, is "a critical theory of *religious* insight" fully concerned with insights arising from the play and confrontation of the world religions? Or does this theory ultimately intend an identification between the "religious" and the Jewish and Christian traditions alone? In other words, despite claims regarding a certain sensitivity to the plurality and ambiguity of theory, culture, and religion, isn't a critical theory of religious insight rooted in a rather narrow, parochial vision of things? One centred upon the predominance of western culture in general, and the Jewish and Christian religions in particular? Why insist on calling it a critical theory of "religious" insight rather than a critical theory of "Judeo-Christian" insight? Wouldn't that title be more accurate and honest?

To respond affirmatively, since the key ideas, themes, and intellectual heritage at work within critical theory stem from modern western culture and history—including Jewish and Christian influences—then a critical theory of religious insight is solidly western and "Judeo-Christian." Perhaps another kind of theory could avoid these constraints. However, a critical theory of religious insight cannot insofar that it intends to contribute to the kind of critical theory that winds its way from Hegel, Feuerbach, and Marx, through to the Frankfurt School, Jürgen Habermas and beyond. Why pretend otherwise? It is clear that the very discipline of critical theory; the particular dilemmas it seeks to redress; and the potential contribution of religious ideas, themes, terms, languages to that theory, largely emerge in relation to the modern/postmodern western world. No critical thinker—religious or otherwise—who endeavours to build upon this theory can fail to engage the historico-cultural specifics of its articulation. It is also for this reason that the place and plight of Judaism and Christianity take on special significance within this complex of concerns. In the final analysis, a critical theory of religious insight is mostly western, monotheistic, and "Judeo-Christian" *as* critical: such is the nature of the beast.

To respond negatively, this historico-cultural characterization—however dominant it may be—can hardly be said to drain the potential form and content of a critical theory of religious insight. In view of the post-religious, post-Christian developments that mark the present time, it is impossible to be untouched or unmoved by the various world religions that are currently shaping the socio-cultural landscape. Nor can one disregard how this multi-religious presence illuminates the plurality and plasticity of each single tradition in itself; of how this exposure conjures up new interpretations, explanations, and applications of the traditions involved; and of the release of diverse religious contents quite beyond their original cultural containers. It would be wrong to suggest, then, that only Judaism and Christianity could contribute to the development of a critical theory of religious insight. Indeed, there is nothing in principle nor in practice that could prevent the articulation of a critical theory informed by the Buddhist or Islamic or Native North American religious traditions, etc. As I see it, it is the task of scholars working within these particular fields of study to take up the critical-theoretic assignment if they find it helpful to do so. However in that event, there are some elemental consequences that are apt to follow.

First, we are likely to witness the genuine pull of religious contents across the board; that is, a reciprocal appreciation and adoption of assorted religious ideas, expressions, terms, doctrines, etc. for the purposes of cultivating the theory. Boundaries between some religious traditions will become highly porous at this level of study. As a result, a critical theory of religious insight could very well embrace the influx of non-western religious contents. Herein lies the potential to develop the theory in other forms—forms that could add to or outstrip what has been suggested in these pages. Of this there can be no doubt. Yet this is not the whole story.

Second, it follows that non-western religious traditions will need to be examined and understood as exposed sub-cultures within a much larger, more powerful modern/postmodern western secular culture. There can be no question of holding to a tradition that, as non-western, is thought to evade such inspection. The concerns that arise here are: what kind of response will this post-religious circumstance evoke from the tradition(s) involved? What kind of self-understanding will it disclose? What kind of religious identity might it affect? What kind of resistance? What forms of accommodation? And what types of theoretical responses will emerge from all of this?

Lastly, the fragmentation and unplanned circulation of the non-western traditions within western culture will have to be mapped out. How wide spread is this fragmentation? How deeply have its shards penetrated into contemporaneity? What might be the critical effect of these particular fragments as opposed to others upon the development of critical religious thought today? Answers here will come with the observation and reflection upon religious phenomena with the potential for critical insight.

These ramifications are hardly transparent goods in themselves, and thus, may not be welcomed by all religious thinkers. Yet if they are embraced—or even if a portion of the project is constructively pursued—then we might witness the proliferation of multiple critical theories of religious insight. This would be a good thing: the very notion of critical theory could only be enriched by such a development. *However, this does not mean that all such theories would be of equal weight or value in relation to the critique of the present.* Some efforts might contribute to the critical transformation of things in a more thorough way than others; in a more provocative way than others; in a more perceptive way than others. A critical theory of religious insight must demonstrate real explanatory power in relation to the range of problems and difficulties facing the contemporary world. Short of this kind of consideration, a critical theory of religious insight might fail to cut through the anti-religious ballast that impedes western thought from exploring unanticipated openings in theory and practice. Thus, not all religious insights arising from every religious tradition will prove critically productive.

It must be made clear that this particular measure of things does not level any normative judgment against the different religious traditions alive on the contemporary scene. The critical-theoretic effectiveness or ineffectiveness of some religious traditions (or facets thereof) neither positively nor negatively accrues to the religions themselves. A critical theory of religious insight is, in this regard, *highly parasitic*. This is to say, it relies upon existing religious traditions and their positive cultivation and communication by a community of dedicated adherents. While this community may be sensitive to the authenticity or moral value of their tradition in relation to others, the critical religious thinker is not. A critical theory of religious insight takes and uses the religious contents that are literally "ex-pressed" by the different world religions under changed historical and socio-cultural conditions. Here it is a question of assessing critical effectiveness rather than metaphysical truthfulness. The theory is therefore unconcerned to actively shape the religious traditions involved; to positively contribute to their religious self-understanding or identity; or to delve into the details of a bona fide communal structure.

Granted, a critical theory of religious insight may generate negative practical and/or theoretical consequences for the traditions under study insofar that the reflexive handling of religious themes, ideas, and terms will critically rebound upon the primary traditions themselves. After all, once religious contents are reflexively shown to be limited, imperfect, divergent, or alterable, they may change. Parasitic or no, then, a critical theory of religious insight hardly lives above the fray. Now, I suppose one could argue that this engagement bears witness to the unfolding of a contemporary form of religious consciousness. Without totally denying this prospect, its diffuse character rather points toward something less formative and more extraneous: namely, the exploratory effort to discern how the fragments of religion might help to enlarge upon the shape, content, and direction of contemporary critical thought.

Bibliography

Abbey, Ruth. *Charles Taylor*. Princeton: Princeton University Press, 2000.

Altizer, Thomas J.J., and William Hamilton. *Radical Theology and the Death of God*. New York: Bobbs-Merrill Company, 1966.

Arac, Jonathan, ed. *After Foucault: Humanistic Knowledge, Postmodern Challenges*. New Brunswick and London: Rutgers University Press, 1988.

Bakhtin, Mikhail. *Problems of Dostoevsky's Poetics*. Translated by Caryl Emerson. Minneapolis: University of Minnesota Press, 1984.

Bauman, Zygmunt. *Modernity and the Holocaust*. Cambridge: Polity Press, 1989.

Baum, Gregory. *Compassion and Solidarity: The Church for Others*. Montréal: CBC Enterprises, 1987.
——— *Theology and Society*. New York: Paulist Press, 1987.
——— "Theories of Post-Modernity," *The Ecumenist* 29 (1991): 4–12.

Benhabib, Selya, Wolfgang Boneß, and John McCole, eds. *On Max Horkheimer: New Perspectives*. Cambridge, Mass.: MIT Press, 1993.

Berman, Russell A. *Modern Culture and Critical Theory: Art, Politics, and the Legacy of the Frankfurt School*. Madison, WI: University of Wisconsin Press, 1989.

Bernstein, Richard. *The New Constellation: The Ethico-Political Horizons of Modernity/Postmodernity*. Cambridge, Mass.: MIT Press, 1991.

Braun, Lev. *Witness to Decline; Albert Camus: Moralist of the Absurd*. Rutherford N.J.: Fairleigh Dickinson University Press, 1974.

Bronner, Stephen. *Camus: Portrait of a Moralist*. Minneapolis: University of Minnesota Press, 1999.

Buber, Martin. *Between Man and Man*. Translated by Ronald Gregor Smith. New York: Macmillan, 1965.
——— *I and Thou*. Translated by Walter Kaufmann. New York: Charles Scribner's Sons, 1970.

Berger, Peter L. *The Sacred Canopy*. Garden City, NY: Doubleday Anchor Books, 1967.

Burggraeve, Roger. *From Self-Development to Solidarity: An Ethical Reading of Human Desire in its Socio-Political Relevance According to Levinas*. Leuven: Peters, 1985.

Calhoun, Craig. *Critical Social Theory: Culture, History, and the Challenge of Difference*. Oxford: Blackwell, 1995.

Camus, Albert. *L'Homme Révolté*. Paris: Gallimard, 1951.
——— *The Rebel: An Essay on Man in Revolt*. Translated by Anthony Bower. New York: Vintage Books, 1956.
——— *The Plague*. Translated by Stuart Gilbert. New York: Vintage, 1984.

Capps, Walter H. *Religious Studies: The Making of a Discipline*. Minneapolis: Fortress Press, 1995.

Cohen, Richard A., ed. *Face to Face with Levinas*. Albany, NY: SUNY, 1986.

Crossan, John Dominic. *The Dark Interval: Towards a Theology of Story*. Allen, TX: Argus, 1975.

Davidson, Arnold J. "Archaeology, Genealogy, Ethics." In *Foucault: A Critical Reader*, edited by David Couzens Hoy. Oxford: Basil Blackwell, 1986.

Davis, Charles. *Temptations of Religion*. New York: Harper and Row, 1973.
——— "The Reconvergence of Theology and Religious Studies." *Studies in Religion/Sciences Religieuses* 4 (1974–75): 205–221.
——— *Theology and Political Society*. Cambridge: Cambridge University Press, 1980.
——— "Wherein There is No Ectasy." *Studies in Religion/Scienes Religieuses*

13 (1984): 393–400.

——— *What is Living, What is Dead in Christianity Today? Breaking the Liberal-Conservative Deadlock*. San Francisco: Harper and Row, 1986.

——— *Soft Bodies in a Hard World: Spirituality for the Vulnerable*. Toronto: Anglican Book Centre, 1987.

——— "Our Modern Identity: The Formation of the Self." *Modern Theology* 6 (1990): 159–171.

——— *Religion and the Making of Society*. Cambridge: Cambridge University Press, 1994.

Dawson, Lorne. "Neither Nerve nor Ectasy: Comment on the Wiebe-Davis Exchange." *Studies in Religion/Sciences Religieuses* 15 (1986): 145–151.

Deleuze, Gilles. "Nomad Thought." In *The New Nietzsche*, edited by David B. Allison. Cambridge, Mass.: MIT Press, 1985.

Despland, Michel. *Reading an Erased Code: Romantic Religion and Literary Aesthetics in France*. Toronto: University of Toronto Press, 1994.

Eagleton, Terry. *The Significance of Theory*. Oxford: Basil Blackwell, 1990.

Emberly, Peter C. *Divine Hunger: Canadians on a Spiritual Walkabout*. Toronto: HarperCollins, 2002.

Fackenheim, Emil L. *God's Presence in History: Jewish Affirmations and Philosophical Reflections*. New York: Harper Torchbooks, 1972.

Fierro, Alfredo. *The Militant Gospel: A Critical Introduction of Political Theologies*. Translated by John Drury. Maryknoll, NY: Orbis Books, 1977.

Foucault, Michel. *Language, Counter-Memory, Practice: Selected Essays and Interviews*. Translated by Donald F. Bouchard and Sherry Simon. Ithaca, NY: Cornell University Press, 1977.

——— *Discipline and Punish: The Birth of the Prison*. Translated by Alan Sheridan. New York: Vintage Books, 1979.

——— *Power/Knowledge: Selected Interviews and Other Writings*. Translated by Colin Gordon, Leo Marshall, John Mepham, and Kate Soper. New York: Pantheon Books, 1980.

—— *The Foucault Reader*. Edited by Paul Rabinow. New York: Pantheon Books, 1984.
—— *Ethics: Subjectivity and Truth*. Vol. One of *The Essential Works of 1954–1984*. Edited by Paul Rabinow. Translated by Robert Hurley and others. New York: The New Press, 1997.

Frankl, Viktor E. *Man's Search for Meaning: An Introduction to Logotherapy*. Translated by Ilse Lasch. New York: Washington Square Press, 1959.

Fraser, Nancy. *Unruly Practices: Power Discourse and Gender in Contemporary Social Theory*. Minneapolis: University of Minnesota Press, 1989.

Freud, Sigmund. *The Future of an Illusion*. Translated by James Strachey. New York: Norton, 1989.

Furrow, Dwight. *Against Theory: Continental and Analytic Challenges in Moral Philosophy*. New York: Routledge, 1995.

Gagnon, Bernard. *La Philosophie Morale et Politique de Charles Taylor*. Québec: Les Presses de l'Université Laval, 2002.

Gardiner, Michael. *The Dialogics of Critique: M.M. Bahktin and the Theory of Ideology*. London: Routledge, 1992.

Griffin, David Ray, William A. Beardslee, and Joe Holland. *Varieties of Postmodern Theology*. Albany, NY: SUNY Press, 1989.

Gutierrez, Gustavo. *A Theology of Liberation: History, Politics, and Salvation*. Translated by Sister Caridad Inda and John Eagleson. Maryknoll, NY: Orbis Books, 1988.

Habermas, Jürgen. *Knowledge and Human Interests*. Translated by Jeremy Shapiro. Boston: Beacon Press, 1971.
—— *Communication and the Evolution of Society*. Translated by Thomas McCarthy. Boston: Beacon Press, 1979.
—— *Philosophical-Political Profiles*. Translated by Frederick G. Lawrence. Cambridge, Mass.: MIT Press, 1983.
—— "Modernity—An Incomplete Project." In *The Anti-Aesthetic: Essays*

on Postmodern Culture, edited by Hal Foster. Port Townsend, Washington: Bay Press, 1983.

——— *The Philosophical Discourse of Modernity: Twelve Lectures*. Translated by Frederick Lawrence. Cambridge, Mass.: MIT Press, 1987.

——— *The New Conservatisim: Cultural Criticism and the Historians' Debate*. Translated by Shierry Weber Nicholson. Cambridge, Mass.: MIT Press, 1989.

——— *Postmetaphysical Thinking: Philosophical Essays*. Translated by Mark Hohengarten. Cambridge, Mass.: MIT Press, 1992.

——— "Transcendence from Within, Transcendence in this World." In *Habermas, Modernity, and Public Theology*. Edited by Don S. Browning and Francis Schüssler Fiorenza. New York: Crossroad, 1992.

——— *Justification and Application: Remarks on Discourse Ethics*. Translated by Ciaran P. Cronin. Cambridge, Mass.: MIT Press, 1993.

Hacking, Ian. "The Archaeology of Foucault." In *Foucault: A Critical Reader*, edited by David Couzens Hoy. Oxford: Basil Blackwell, 1986.

Hall, Douglas John. *The End of Christendom and the Future of Christianity*. Eugene, Oregon: Wipf and Stock Publishers, 1997.

Hart, Kevin. *The Trespass of the Sign: Deconstruction, Theology, and Philosophy*. Cambridge: Cambridge University Press, 1989.

Helm, Thomas E. *The Christian Religion: An Introduction*. Englewood Cliffs, N.J.: Prentice Hall, 1991.

Heyde, Ludwig. *The Weight of Finitude: On the Philosophical Question of God*. Translated by Alexander Harmsen and William Desmond. Albany, NY: SUNY Press, 1999.

Holquist, Michael. *Dialogism: Bakhtin and His World*. London: Routledge, 1990.

Horkheimer, Max. *Kritische Theorie*. Band II. Frankfurt am Main: Fischer Verlag, 1968.

——— *Critical Theory: Selected Essays*. Translated by Matthew J. O'Connell and others. New York: Continuum, 1972.

——— "Foreword" to *The Dialectical Imagination: A History of the Frankfurt School and the Institute of Social Research, 1923–1950*, by Martin Jay. Berkeley: University of California Press, 1973.
——— *Between Philosophy and the Social Sciences: Selected Early Writings*. Translated by G. Frederick Hunter, Matthew S. Kramer, and John Torpey. Cambridge, Mass.: MIT Press, 1993.

Horkheimer, Max and Theodor W. Adorno. *Dialektik der Aufklärung: Philosophische Fragmente*. Amsterdam: Querido, 1947.
——— *Dialectic of Enlightenment*. Translated by John Cumming. New York: Continuum, 1990.

Hoy, David Couzens, ed. *Foucault: A Critical Reader*. Oxford: Basil Blackwell, 1986.
——— "Foucault: Modern or Postmodern?" In *After Foucault: Humanistic Knowledge, Postmodern Challenges*, edited by Jonathan Arac. New Brunswick: Rutgers University Press, 1988.

Huges, H. Stuart. *Consiousness and Society: The Reconstruction of European Social Thought, 1890–1930*. New York: Vintage, 1961.

Huyssen, Andreas. *After the Great Divide: Modernism, Mass Culture, Postmodernism*. Bloomington: Indiana University Press, 1986.

Jameson, Fredric. 1983 "Postmodernism and Consumer Society." In *The Anti-Aesthetic: Essays on Postmodern Culture*, edited by Hal Foster. Port Townsend, Washington: Bay Press, 1983.
——— "Forward" to *The Postmodern Condition: A Report on Knowledge*, by Jean-François Lyotard. Translated by Geoff Bennington and Brian Massumi. Minneapolis: University of Minnesota Press, 1984.
——— *Postmodernism, Or, the Cultural Logic of Late Capitalism*. Durham: Duke University Press, 1991.

Jay, Martin. *The Dialectical Imagination: A History of the Frankfurt School and the Institute of Social Research, 1923–1950*. Berkeley: University of California Press, 1973.

Kearny, Richard and Emmanuel Levinas. "Dialogue with Emmanuel Levinas."

In *Face to Face with Levinas*, edited by Richard Cohen. Albany, NY: SUNY, 1986.

Kellner, Douglas. *Critical Theory, Marxism and Modernity*. Baltimore: Johns Hopkins University Press, 1989.

Kee, Alistar. *Marx and the Failure of Liberation Theology*. London: SCM Press, 1990.

Kroeker, P. Travis. "The Ironic Cage of Positivism and the Nature of Philosophical Theology." *Studies in Religion/Sciences Religieuses* 22 (1993): 93–103.
——— "Reply to Donald Wiebe." *Studies in Religion/Sciences Religieuses* 23 (1994):

Kropp, Bettina L., ed. *Critical Essays on ALbert Camus*. Boston: G.K. Hall, 1998.

Küng, Hans and David Tracy, eds. *Paradigm Change in Theology: A Symposium for the Future*. New York: Crossroad, 1989.

Lalonde, Marc P. ed. *The Promise of Critical Theology: Essays in Honour of Charles Davis*, edited by Marc P. Lalonde. Waterloo, Ontario: Wilfrid Laurier University Press, 1995.
——— *Critical Theology and the Challenge of Jürgen Habermas: Toward a Critical Theory of Religious Insight*. New York: Peter Lang, 1999.

Levinas, Emmanuel. *Totality and Infinity: An Essay on Exteriority*. Translated by Alphonso Lingis. Pittsburgh: Duquesne University Press, 1969.
——— *Otherwise than Being: Or, Beyond Essence*. Translated by Alphonso Lingis. The Hague: Martinus Nijhoff, 1981.
——— "God and Philosophy." In *The Levinas Reader*, edited by Seán Hand. Oxford: Basil Blackwell, 1989.
——— "Judaism and Kenosis." In *In the Time of the Nations*. Translated by Michael B. Smith. Bloomington: Indiana University Press, 1994.

Lossky, Vladimir. *In the Image and Likeness of God*. Crestwood, NY: St. Vladimir Seminary Press, 1974.

Lundin, Roger, Anthony C. Thiselton, and Clarence Walhout. *The Responsibility of Hermeneutics*. Grand Rapids, MI: Wm. B. Eerdmans Publishing Company, 1985.

Lunn, Eugene. *Marxism and Modernism: An Historical Study of Lukács, Brecht, Bemjamin and Adorno*. Berkeley: Unniverstity of California Press, 1982.

Marion, Jean-Luc. *God Without Being*. Translated by Thomas A. Carlson. Chicago: University of Chicago Press, 1991.

Marx, Wener. *Towards a Phenomenology of Ethics: Ethos and the Life-World*. Translated by Ashraf Noor. Albany, NY: SUNY Press, 1992.

McBrien, Richard P. *Catholicism: Study Edition*. San Francisco: Harper and Row, 1981.

McCann, Dennis P. *Christian Realism and Liberation Theology: Practical Theologies in Creative Conflict*. Maryknoll, NY: Orbis Books, 1981.

McCarthy, Patrick. *Camus: A Critical Study of His Life and Work*. London: Hamish Hamilton, 1982.

Meagher, John C. *The Truing of Christianity: Visions of Life and Thought for the Future*. New York: Doubleday, 1990.

Merton, Thomas. *Albert Camus' The Plague*. New York: Seabury Press, 1968.

Metz, J.B. *Faith in History and Society: Toward a Practical Fundamental Theology*. Translated by David Smith. New York: Crossroad, 1980.

Milbank, John. *Theology and Social Theory: Beyond Secular Reason*. Oxford: Basil Blackwell, 1990.

Milbank, John, Catherine Pickstock, and Graham Ward, eds. *Radical Orthodoxy: A New Theology*. London: Routledge, 1999.

Montaigne, Michel de. *Essays*. Translated by J.M. Cohen. London: Penguin, 1958.

Nagel, Thomas. *The View From Nowhere*. New York: Oxford University Press, 1986.

Norris, Christopher. *Deconstruction: Theory and Practice*. London: Routledge, 1982.
——— "Deconstruction, Postmodernism and Philosophy: Habermas on Derrida." In *Derrida: A Critical Reader*, edited by David Wood. Oxford: Basil Blackwell, 1992.

Peillon, Michael. *The Concept of Interest in Social Theory*. Lewiston, NY: Edwin Mellen Press, 1990.

Pélaby, Janie. *Charles Taylor: Penseur de la Pluralité*. Ste. Foy: Presses de l'Univesité Laval, 2001.

Peukert, Helmut. *Science, Action, and Fundamental Theology: Toward a Theology of Communicative Action*. Translated by James Bohman. Cambridge, Mass.: MIT Press, 1986.

Poster, Mark. *Critical Theory and Poststructuralism: In Search of A Context* Ithaca, NY: Cornell University Press, 1989.

Rajchman, John. "Habermas' Complaint." *New German Critique* 45 (1988): 103–114.

Remus, Harold, William Closson James and Daniel Fraikin. *Religious Studies in Ontario: A State-of-the-Art Review*. Waterloo, Ontario: Wilfrid Laurier University Press, 1992.

Richard, Lucien. "The Possibility of the Incarnation According to Emmanuel Levinas." *Studies in Religion/Sciences Religieuses* 17 (1988): 391–405.

Ricouer, Paul. *A Ricouer Reader: Reflection and Imagination*. Edited by Mario J. Valdés. Toronto: University of Toronto Press, 1991.

Rosenstock-Heussy, Eugen. *Speech and Reality*. Norwich, Vt: Argo Books. 1970.

Saler, Benson. *Conceptualizing Religion: Immanent Anthropologists, Transcendent Natives, and Unbounded Categories*. New York: E.J. Brill, 1993.

Schnädelbach, Herbert. "Max Horkheimer and the Philosophy of German Idealism." In *On Max Horkheimer: New Perspectives*, edited by Selya Benhabib, Wolfgang Bonß, and John McCole. Cambridge, Mass: MIT Press, 1993.

Siebert, Rudolf. *The Critical Theory of Religion: The Frankfurt School. From Universal Pragmatic to Political Theology*. New York: Mouton, 1985.
——— *From Critical Theory to Communicative Political Theology: Universal Solidarity*. New York: Peter Lang, 1989.

Smith, Nicholas H. *Charles Taylor: Meaning, Morals, and Modernity*. Cambridge: Polity, 2002.

Smith, Wilfred Cantwell. *The Meaning and End of Religion: A New Approach to the Religious Traditions of Mankind*. New York: Mentor Books, 1964.

Spivey, Robert. "Modest Messiahs: The Study of Religion in State Universities." *Religious Education* 63 (1968): 5–12.

Sprintzen, David. *Camus: A Critical Examination*. Philadelphia: Temple University Press, 1988.

Taylor, Charles. "What is Human Agency?" In *Human Agency and Language*. Cambridge: Cambridge University Press, 1985.
——— "Foucault on Freedom and Truth." In *Foucault: A Critical Reader*, edited by David Couzens Hoy Oxford: Basil Blackwell, 1986.
——— *Sources of the Self: The Making of the Modern Identity*. Cambridge, Mass.: Harvard U.P., 1989.
——— "Language and Society." In *Communicative Action: Essays on Jürgen Habermas' Theory of Communicative Action*, edited by Axel Honneth and Hans Joas. Translated by Jeremy Gaines and Doris L. Jones. Cambridge, Mass.: MIT Press, 1991.
——— "Reply and Re-articulation." In *Philosophy in an Age of Pluralism: The Philosophy of Charles Taylor in Question*, edited by James E. Tully. Cambridge: Cambridge University Press, 1994.

―――― *Philosophical Arguments*. Cambridge, Mass.: Harvard U.P., 1995.
―――― *A Catholic Modernity?* New York: Oxford, 1999.

Taylor, Mark C. *Erring: A Postmodern A/Theology*. Chicago: University of Chicago Press, 1984.
―――― "Postmodern Times." In *The Otherness of God*, edited by Orrin F. Summerell. Charlottesville: University of Virginia Press, 1998.

Tillich, Paul. *The Courage to Be*. London: Collins, 1952.

Todorov, Tzvetan. *Mikhail Bakhtin: The Dialogical Principle*. Translated by Wlad Godzich. Minneapolis: University of Minnesota Press, 1984.

Tully, James E., ed. *Philsosophy in an Age of Pluralism: The Philosophy of Charles Taylor in Question*. Cambridge: Cambridge University Press, 1994.

Visker, Rudi. "Habermas on Heidegger and Foucault: Meaning and Validity in *The Philosophical Discourse of Modernity*." *Radical Philosophy* 61 (1992): 15–22.

Walzer, Michael. "The Politics of Michel Foucault." In *Foucault: A Critical Reader*, edited by David Couzens Hoy. Oxford: Basil Blackwell, 1986.

Watson, Stephen H. *Extentions: Essays on Interpretation, Rationality, and the Closure of Modernism*. Albany, NY: State University of New York Press, 1992.

Weber, Max. *Economy and Society*. Vol. 1. New York: Bedminster Press, 1968.

Wiebe, Donald. "The Failure of Nerve in the Academic Study of Religion." *Studies in Religion/Scienes Religieuses* 13 (1984): 402–422.
―――― *The Irony of Theology and the Nature of Religious Thought*. Kingston and Montreal: McGill-Queen's University Press, 1991.
―――― "Argument or Authority in the Academy? On Kroeker on *The Irony of Theology*." *Studies in Religion/Scienes Religieuses* 23 (1993): 67–79.

Wigggershaus, Rolf. *The Frankfurt School: Its History, Theories, and Political*

Significance. Translated by Michael Robertson. Cambridge, Mass.: MIT Press, 1995.

Williams, Bernard. *Moral Luck*. Cambridge: Cambridge University Press, 1981.

Wolin, Sheldon S. "On the Theory and Practice of Power." In *After Foucault: Humanistic Knowledge, Postmodern Challenges*, edited by Jonathan Arac. New Brunswick and London: Rutgers University Press, 1988.

Wyschogrod, Edith. *Emmanuel Levinas: The Problem of Ethical Metaphysics*. The Hague: Martinus Nijhoff, 1974.
——— "Man-Made Mass Death: Shifting Concepts of Community." *Journal of the American Academy of Religion* 58 (1990): 165–176.

Yannaras, Christos. *The Freedom of Morality*. Translated by Elizabeth Briere. Crestwood, NY: St. Valdimir's Seminary Press, 1984.

Index

Adorno, Theodor, 5, 48–49, 70, 84
alterity, 17, 19–21, 25, 93
articulation, 88–89

Bakhtin, Mikhail, 68
Baum, Gregory, 30, 39
Berger, Peter, 38
Bernstein, Richard, 55
best account, 83, 90, 91, 94
Blanchot, Maurice, 20

Calhoun, Craig, 45, 68, 69
Camus, Albert, 12, 66, 70–74, 86
communicative action, 5, 6, 49
community, 20, 36, 40, 65, 69, 103
compassion, 6, 47, 56, 57, 74, 82, 83–88, 90, 96
Crossan, John Dominic, 39

Davis, Charles, 3, 9–10, 15–16, 21–26, 33, 34, 46, 73
Derrida, Jacques, 20, 54, 55
dialectic, 17, 18, 66–70
dialectic of enlightenment, 48–49, 57
deconstruction, 18–19, 22, 26, 54–56
domination, 6, 18, 30, 31, 34, 39, 40, 41

eclecticism, 16
ethics, 52, 58, 59, 82, 92, 93

emancipation, 29, 33, 35–36, 38, 49, 54, 56
emancipatory interest, 10, 18, 29, 30, 40

face, the, 58, 92
faith, 3, 4, 7, 10, 18, 22, 23, 24, 33, 34, 38, 45, 46, 58, 60, 65, 66, 69, 70, 72, 74, 95
Fackenheim, Emil, 24
Feuerbach, Ludwig, 101
Foucault, Michel, 3, 10, 11, 29–41, 47, 50–52, 82, 88, 94
fragmentation, 7, 11, 12, 40, 54, 67, 69, 70, 82, 88, 94, 95, 102, 104
Fraikin, Daniel, 48
Frankl, Viktor, 47
Frankfurt School, 1, 2, 12, 29, 41, 49, 101

Gardiner, Michael, 68
God, 8, 12, 18, 24–25, 30, 39–40, 46, 55, 58, 59, 71, 73, 74–75, 83, 85, 91–95
Griffin, David Ray, 18–21, 22, 25
Guide, André, 69
Gutierrez, Gustavo, 29, 30, 36

Habermas, Jürgen, 1, 2, 5, 11, 17, 29, 32, 47, 49, 52–59, 83, 84, 85, 101
Hall, Douglas John, 4

Hegel, G.W.F., 101
Horkheimer, Max, 12, 48–49, 52, 83–88, 90, 91, 93, 95
Hoy, David Couzens, 36
humanism, exclusivist, 12, 66, 71–74
Huyssen, Andreas, 16, 17

identity, 3, 4, 15, 17, 20, 21, 23, 52, 67, 70, 81, 102, 103
ideology-critique, 33, 40, 69
injustice, 6, 29, 36, 39, 71–73, 83, 85, 87, 90, 93, 95
instrumental reason, 49

James, William Closson, 48
Jameson, Frederic, 16
Jewish thought, modern, 5, 95
justice, 19, 70, 71, 74, 91, 92, 93, 94, 95

Kant, Immanuel, 50
kenosis, 73, 82, 86, 91
Küng, Hans, 15

Levinas, Emmanuel, 11, 12, 20, 47, 52, 57–60, 73, 83, 87, 91–95
Lossky, Vladimir, 66, 67
love, 6, 23–26, 32, 40, 58, 66, 70–75, 86–87, 90, 91
Lunn, Eugene, 69
Lyotard, Jean-François, 20

Marx, Karl, 2, 29, 101
Marx, Werner, 68, 69

Materialism, 30, 85
Mauss, Marcel, 30
meontology, 57, 58, 59
metaphysics, 15, 21, 22, 23, 26, 36, 70, 74, 84, 85, 87, 90, 103
modernism, 69
modernity, 29, 35, 41, 48, 49, 51, 53, 54, 66
Montaigne, Michel de, 68
morality, 12, 56, 70, 85–91

neoconservative, 16, 17, 19, 22, 25, 26
Nietzsche, Friedrich, 54, 55, 58, 81, 86
nihilism, 6, 21–22, 26, 38, 49, 69
normative, 10, 16, 18, 31, 32, 52, 70, 83, 103
Norris, Christopher, 55, 56
orthodoxy, 10, 23–26
Other, the, 20, 57–59, 72, 75, 86–87, 91–96
otherness, 15, 17–18, 20, 21, 25, 57, 70, 82, 91

parabolic, 10, 39–41
particularity, 9, 10, 24—25, 26, 65, 70, 75, 81, 89
pluralism, 15, 22, 50
power, 6, 8, 10, 29–41, 49, 86, 87, 92, 93
post-Christian, 4, 82, 83, 95, 101
post-Enlightenment, 9
postmetaphysics, 52–57, 84, 85, 82–89

postmodernism, 1, 4, 5, 6, 9, 10, 11, 16–22, 25, 26, 29, 47, 52, 54–56
postorthodoxy, 9, 10, 15, 16, 21–26, 67
post-Religious, 7–9, 11, 65–75, 101–102

rebellion, 12, 34, 36, 71–72
religious studies, 5, 10, 11, 45–53, 59, 60
religious thought, 1–13, 15–16, 21, 22, 25, 65–66, 71, 75, 81–82, 94, 96, 102
Remus, Harold, 48
revolution, 30, 33, 36, 59
Rossenstock-Heussy, Eugen, 32

Saler, Benson, 67
Same, the, 91, 93, 95
secularism, 4–9, 13, 25, 51, 54, 65–66, 69, 75, 81–82, 83, 102
Smith, Wilfred Cantwell, 67, 68, 69
Spivey, Robert, 47, 48
Strenki, Ivan, 48
strong evaluation, 88, 90
supernatural, 51, 58, 65

Taylor, Charles, 8, 12, 29, 48, 68, 74, 75, 83, 88–91
Taylor, Mark C., 18, 20, 21, 22, 25
theology: a/theology, 10, 18, 20, 22; critical theology, 1–5, 9; death of God theology, 4; liberation theology, 3, 10, 29–41; political theology, 34, 41; postmodern theology, 10, 15, 18–21, 22, 25

theory: critical theory, 1–9, 11, 12, 13, 30, 74, 82–88, 90, 93, 94–95, 96, 101, 102, 103; critical theory of religious insight, 1, 5–9, 11, 12, 13, 59, 81–96, 101–104
totality, 24, 70, 71
Tracy, David, 15
transgression, 9, 10, 11, 12, 38, 40, 47, 50–52, 57–60, 66, 74–75
transcendence, 23, 26, 38, 39, 54, 71, 72, 93
truth, 4, 11, 18, 19, 21, 22, 23, 24, 29, 31–32, 33, 34, 37, 45, 46, 47, 51, 52, 65, 84, 85, 88, 89, 93

Weber, Max, 37, 38
Wyschogrod, Edith, 20–21, 25